Look at Me,
I can Read at 3

Look at Me, I can Read at 3

A step-by-step guide to teaching your 3-year-old to Read and Write

Gheda Ismail

Library of Congress Control Number:		2012903813
ISBN:	Hardcover	978-1-4653-0144-4
	Softcover	978-1-4653-0143-7
	Ebook	978-1-4628-4989-5

To order additional copies of this book, contact:
Xlibris Corporation
1-800-618-969
www.Xlibris.com.au
Orders@Xlibris.com.au
500629

Contents

Chapter 1

All You Need to Know Before You Start

[For the purpose of this book the female gender has been used to refer to the child.]

You are reading this book for a reason. You have picked up this book with the slightest hope that maybe what the front cover suggests is true. Is it possible for a child as young as 3 to read? Can a young child learn from a parent, without any teaching qualifications? Is it possible for a child to be well ahead in her reading and writing even before she enters school?

The answer is yes. If you have high expectations of a child, then she will succeed. Likewise, if you believe that all a child is good for is playing, then that's basically all she will do.

It is possible for a child as young as 3 to read and write because my daughter is living proof. And everything she knows is because of what I have taught her. She has never attended a child care centre or any other lessons apart from the work I have done with her at home.

My daughter loves to read. We sit together every day and she chooses a book from the many books she has. She is a fluent reader, sounding out unfamiliar words and reading sight words she has memorised from memory. She stops at full stops and raises her voice when she approaches exclamation marks. Currently she is reading at level 20. This is considered a reading age of an 8-year old child. She is now aged 4 years and 5 months. She will be school age next year. In addition, she is a fluent writer, and can easily write a full page story or recount with minimal assistance.

Below is a 2-page spread of what a level 20 book looks like. And what follows it is a sample of her writing aged 4 years and 4 months.

As she ran down the last hill,
Alex saw Mum
standing among the other parents.
Then she saw Dad!
He had come, after all!

Olivia was still in the lead
but she wasn't too far ahead.
Alex knew that this was the moment
to speed up.

She ran faster
than she had ever run before.
She tried so hard
that she ran past Olivia
and hit the tape first.

The Running Shoes by Angelique Filleul, 2002, reprinted with the permission of Cengage Learning Australia Pty Ltd.

Sample of Halima's writing aged 4 years and 4 months.

Halima Awwad
The silly boy.
It was sunday and Tim was
playing with his toys.
Then mam called time
to have lunch.
But Tim didnt want
to go downstairs
I'm busy Tim said.
OK said mam.
So mam and dad
had lunch on their
own then Tim got
very hungry so he
went downstairs
sorry said mam there
is no more food left
Tim was sad

Ok, Halima is a child. A very young child. But she can read and write.

She is, however, a normal kid. She has her tantrums. We have food fights. She is familiar with the naughty corner. She is a child. But she can read because she has been taught the basic fundamentals of reading from the age of 3. While there has not been much research on early reading, it is a skill that can be taught to children as young as 3. In addition, a child can also learn the basics of writing and can start to produce her own text soon after. As you know, children are like sponges and absorb the world around them, so if you plan the environment around learning, they will no doubt pick it up.

The Purpose of this Book

The purpose of this book is to teach your child the fundamental skills she will need to attack the goals of reading and writing. Unlike what many people think, children can be taught to read from as early as 3 years of age. Once you have learnt how the process of reading works, and have taught this to your child, then she will be able to read. The level of reading she attains at the end of the Program will depend on a few things—how long you continue with the Program, your child's ability to a certain extent, and the amount of reading material you expose your child to throughout the Program. If you and your child persevere, your child will reach a higher reading level than others who do not.

In this book you will learn the process of teaching your child the *phonics* approach to reading. This alphabetic, phonic approach to teaching reading has been used for centuries. It is the essence of successful reading. The phonic approach is based on two assumptions. One is that the sound of a letter has a relationship to the letter or graphemes. The second is that once children have learned the relationship between the letters and sounds, they can say the printed words by blending the sounds together, or sounding the word out. The teaching of phonics commences with the teaching of the **letters of the alphabet**. Beginning readers need to learn the names of the letters and the sounds of the letters. This can be done by reading alphabet books and pointing out the shapes of the letters and saying the corresponding sound and letter name. It doesn't really matter which way round they are taught. Children can learn the sound and the names at the same time with ease. This Program will give you suggestions on how to do this easily.

Once the letter sounds and names have been mastered it is time to move on to the sounds that two or more letters say together. This is called 'blending'. For example. a-t, a-m, c-a-t and m-a-t.

Lots of practice is needed to make blending smooth and easy. Grouping words into families is the best way to learn to blend in a logical and sequential way. For example, introducing several examples with the same blend such as cat, mat, rat, hat, etc. (Ashton Townsend, 2011)

Children also discover that rules learned in phonics do not apply to every word—that particular letters or combinations of letters may not always be pronounced the same way. Therefore **sight words** need to be introduced to the child in conjunction with phonics.

Sight words are the words that readers should recognise instantly, without having to break up or sound out. Readers should recognise sight words quickly because they are so frequently used in everyday reading and writing. In fact sight words make up 50—75 % of all words that children read. Many sight words do not sound as they are spelled, making them difficult to sound out using knowledge of phonics. This is why memorising sight words gives the child a better chance to tackle more difficult and infrequent words, without losing the meaning of what is being read (Elizabeth, 2011).

Since these sight words (such as *could, who, were,* and *you*) don't follow phonics rules, they have to be studied and memorised. Other high frequency words—such as *it, he, she, them* are also emphasised because this helps increase a student's fluency.

Initially, after teaching your child the fundamental skills of the alphabet and other important skills, your child will be ready for a level 1 reading book. This is what schools begin a child on in Kindergarten, once she has mastered all or most of the alphabet names and sounds. Most schools want a child to be at a reading level 7 or 8 by the end of her first school year (end of Kindergarten). On the following pages are some sample pages of what different reading levels look like. They are from the Nelson Cengage PM Plus Reading Program. As your child progresses through the Program slowly, she will move forward in her reading level as she accomplishes various learning goals.

Sample of Book level 1: Baby

Baby by Annette Smith, Jenny Giles and Beverly Randell, 2000, reprinted with the permission of Cengage Learning Australia Pty Ltd.

Sample of Book level 2: The Toy Box

The Toy Box by Annette Smith, Jenny Giles and Beverly Randell, 2000, reprinted with the permission of Cengage Learning Australia Pty Ltd.

Sample of Book level 3: Teddy Bear's Picnic

"Panda! Panda!

Come in the balloon.

Come to the picnic

in the balloon."

Teddy Bear's Picnic by Beverly Randell, 2000, reprinted with the permission of Cengage Learning Australia Pty Ltd.

Sample of Book Level 4: Bedtime

"My car can go

up and down," said Jack.

"Come on," said Mum.

"Come to bed."

Bedtime by Annette Smith, 2000, reprinted with the permission of Cengage Learning Australia Pty Ltd.

Sample of Book Level 6: Little Chimp Runs Away

Mother Chimp
can not see Little Chimp.
"Come back here,
Little Chimp!
Come back here!"

Little Chimp Runs Away by Jenny Giles, 2000, reprinted with the permission of Cengage Learning Australia Pty Ltd.

Sample of Book Level 8: Katie's caterpillar

"The boys and girls at school
like you, Katie," said Joe.
"Your teacher likes you, too."

"No," said Katie.
"I'm not going back to school."

Katie's Caterpillar by Annette Smith, 2000, reprinted with the permission of Cengage Learning Australia Pty Ltd.

Sample of Book Level 10: Baby Bear's Hiding Place

Baby Bear went into the forest with Father Bear.

"Look at all the red berries in my basket!" said Baby Bear.

"You are a good little bear," said Father Bear.

Baby Bear's Hiding Place by Beverly Randell, 2001, reprinted with the permission of Cengage Learning Australia Pty Ltd.

Sample of Book Level 13: The Crow and the Pot

But the crow was a big bird. His head was too big to get inside the pot.

"I do want a drink," he said. "But I can't put my beak in the water."

The Crow And The Pot by Beverly Randell, 2001, reprinted with the permission of Cengage Learning Australia Pty Ltd.

The Program

What makes this Program so effective is that it is simple and straight forward. It is comprised of a set of easy-to-complete Checklists that are repeated during each learning day. Each Checklist acts as a motivator for you as you attempt to accomplish all the activities prescribed for your child for the day. When you tick all the boxes you will feel a sense of satisfaction and that will drive you to stick to the Program. You will try to complete all activities allocated in the Checklist. You will try not to miss a day. But if you do, it's not a big deal. The Checklists have been created for you so all you need to do is photocopy them and start the Program. The Checklists are also effective in that you do not need to do much planning, as the work is already planned out for you. The only thing you need to do is monitor your child's progress and determine, based on the suggestions given, when it is time for your child to move on to the next Checklist. Each Checklist follows on from the previous one, with some important changes and adjustments as the child continues to make progress.

Each Checklists focus on reading strategies as well as teaching your child to write. It is recommended that you work with your child in both the reading and writing activities, not matter how their fine motor skills are. They will still benefit greatly. However if you just want to focus on the reading activities you can. But what a great joy to see your child write her name at the age of 3, or to be able to sound out and write basic write not long after. So attempt to complete all the activities in the Checklist for maximum benefit.

If you are using the program for a child already at school (in Kindergarten) then your child's fine motor skills may probably be well developed. In this case you may not want to implement the writing/tracing activities in the Checklists. However, having said this, I notice that many children who are struggling in Kindergarten actually have difficulty in their fine motor skills and need more practice with tracing words, letters and numbers. If that's the case then it would make sense to implement the Checklists in whole.

Who is this Book for?

This book has been planned so that parents can take advantage of this Program at various times of their child's early life. This book can is of benefit to:

- ✓ *Parents with babies or toddlers*: This is a great time for parents of young ones to prepare themselves with the process of teaching their child to read and write even before their child is ready. Use the knowledge in this book to gain an insight into the Program so that when the child is 3, you can begin the program immediately.
- ✓ *Parents of 3- and 4-year olds*: Parents with children in this age group can begin the Program outlined in this book straight away using the Checklists and recommended resources. It is recommended to start the Program before your child starts school.
- ✓ *Parents of 5- and 6-year olds*: Parents of Kindergarten and Year 1 children who have not grasped the foundations of literacy in their first year of schooling will find this book of great benefit as they can use the strategies outlined to assist their child go back to the basics of phonics learning. Many parents complain that their child's Kindergarten teacher doesn't identify and relay problems their child is having until the end of the year, or when they reach Year 1. By then the child has missed out on the basics of literacy learning, and they move on to Year 1 struggling. If no intervention is given, the child will continue on the road to failure, as a gap in

their learning from Kindergarten has increased over time. This can take many months or years to rectify. Parents who use the strategies outlined in this book while their child is in Kindergarten, or in the 6 weeks holidays at the end of the Kindergarten, or even in Year 1, can assist their child if they show signals they have problems with literacy.

How Was this Book Born?

When my daughter turned 3, I felted anxious about starting her off on the road to learning. Being a teacher, I felt it was time to assist my daughter to become literate, despite her tiny age of just 3 years old.

So from that day on I began thinking about how I could prepare a program so my daughter can read. Why the hurry to start her off on the road to learning, you think? She was only 3. She was also nowhere near school age. Here's why—I am a mother with learning at the top of my child's agenda. And I'm sure many mothers can relate with that. But most mothers feel intimidated with the idea of teaching their child; they feel it is something specialised that only a qualified teacher can do. But they are wrong.

I googled some ideas about how to go about teaching a 3-year-old to read and write—I didn't get any useful things. I mostly got a bunch of websites about learning the ABCs. Nothing else that progressed from that. It's funny that there really are little expectations of what a 3-year-old can do. They are considered 'bright' if they know their ABCs. Is that all they are capable of? I felt so upset at the lack of resources out there that I decided it was time for me to see what I could come up with myself.

My Background

I finished my Bachelor of Education (Primary) degree at University of Western Sydney in 2005. After working in a few public and private schools while I was completing my degree and after I finished, my husband and I opened up a tutoring business, Step Ahead Coaching. As the business flourished I left my school teaching to pursue the rare opportunity to work for myself, with my husband, in a work environment where I controlled the work load, teaching strategies and basically everything about my work conditions. I am head teacher of my tutoring business until today, eight years on.

So what's this have to do with reading at 3? Well, I have had a fascination with learning, and I'd like to give my daughter the best possible start to life and to school. So all these years of experience in my field have come forth in this book that will hopefully lead you and your child to the successful path of learning at a young age.

My Philosophy

My Philosophy is that the most important learning goes on between a child and a parent. Not between child and DS, or child and TV, or child and Wii. Not even between child and school teacher. This because learning at home assists the child to see links between learning and living, and learning and life. This obviously makes sense as the child spends more of her time at home than any other place. So learning at home would be the obvious step to take.

Be aware that this is not dependent on the family's cultural or socio-economic background. You don't need to be well-off to teach your child, or even have a degree for that matter.

Do You Love Your Child?

What kind of question is this, you may ask? Of course you love your child! You would do anything for her. You would buy anything for her. Anything that would make her happy.

A lot of parents, however, assume they can buy their child's love with fancy toys or games, many of which are ridiculously expensive. Moreover, the child does not appreciate the money that has been spent in the process of obtaining them. But toys do not buy a child's love. Your child will not love you more if you buy her more toys. And you will not love your child more if she is busy with more toys.

However, you have an advantage in this scenario because you have the mental capacity to determine what is best for your child, while your child does not have the brains for that yet. You can make sound decisions about what your child spends her time doing.

But I Don't Have Time!

I often hear from my students' parents that they don't have time to teach their child. The parents are often busy with work. The kids are in front of the TV or other passive form of entertainment. There is cooking and cleaning waiting to get done. There is a husband waiting to get spoilt when he returns from work. There are the supermarket specials luring you to the shops. There are the social outings you have planned and your friends' get-togethers you are looking forward to attending. The list is endless.

And time is flying. Whatever time that goes you cannot get it back. So it now goes back to prioritising. If time is going one way or another, then you need to decide how you want to spend your time so it can be used in the most beneficial way. Do you need to shop everyday or can or can it be done once a week? Do you need to buy the ingredients that you need for your meal now, or can you make a meal with the ingredients you have at home? I'm sure that the latter can be arranged with very little organisation from you. These are just a few examples of small changes you can make in your family' life that can make a difference to the time you have; thus leading to bit more time in the day for you to teach your child.

Ditch the Time Wasters!

If you are lucky enough to have all of your children aged 3 and under then it really is very simple to make a few adjustments to your child's play time and sources of amusement. Your kids won't even notice. TV doesn't have to be a major source of entertainment (I personally haven't kept a television since I got married, about 8 years ago, but that's just me). You can substitute a bit of TV viewing with some shared book reading, or even some colouring in, or blocks. Anything, basically, that doesn't involve passive amusement.

Frederick Zimmerman and Dimitri Christakis at the University of Washington in Seattle, found that kids who watched the most TV before the age of 3 performed poorest on reading and mathematics tests at ages 6 and 7. Kids who watched the least TV had the highest probability of graduating from university by the age of 26, regardless of IQ or socioeconomic status. While those who watched the most TV, more than 3 hours per day, had the highest chance of dropping out of school without qualifications (Gosline, 2005).

I am not going to delve into how to raise your family and how to live your life. This book is about how to help your child read and write at an early age. But in order to do this you need to understand that you may need to change your goals and habits so that learning with your child becomes a priority to you. And that requires you to shift your time focus from one thing to another. To make 30 minutes a day for your child you will need to cut out 30 minutes you and your child spend doing other things, probably things that are of little benefit anyway. Cutting out 30 minutes both you and your child spend watching TV is an example of this.

You may be thinking that I must have all the time in the world. Isn't this how I had the time to create this Program? Well, the fact is, I was very busy when I piloted the Program. I was the Primary Coordinator and teacher of all the primary classes in my business, teaching 6 days a week after school, I had just given birth to my second daughter (who was not an easy baby), and was a superwoman housewife juggling the demands of cooking and cleaning and raising a young family (and no, I didn't have a dishwasher back then, too!)

And to give you a bit of motivation, check out the following link of a video posted on YouTube, showing my daughter Halima aged 3 years 4 months reading sentences. The title of the video is 'Amazing 3 year old child reading sentences.'

http://www.youtube.com/watch?v=dwnSrYLh7EI

Write It Down!

One of the basic fundamentals of this Program is that you have a written record/checklist everyday of what you will be doing with your child. This crystallises your goals and gives them more force. It motivates you to stick to the Program and makes you accountable if you don't.

In 1964, all members of the Harvard Business School graduating class stated that they have, on graduation day, clear goals that they want to achieve in life. Among them, 5% made the time to write them down on paper. A follow up study was done in 1984 and it was discovered that 95% of those who had written down their goals accomplished them within 20 years. Among the "lazy" majority, only 5% of them were able to achieve their expected goals (Fitz Villa Fuerte, 2007).

Writing down goals assists us realise what we are striving for. Many people will decide they want to set a goal and won't actually write it down. They'll keep it in their head where it remains vague and fuzzy and then sooner rather than later, they forget about it as life takes over and they stop working towards it.

Having a Learning Checklist is of vital importance if you want to achieve it. Firstly, it helps you remember that you have set goals for the day. Very few people remember their goals if they don't write them down, because life gets busy and something distracts them and they forget about their goals.

A written record (the Checklists) therefore ensures that you remember your goal. If you write it down and then leave it somewhere that you can see it one or more times a day, then you are going to keep yourself focused on the goal and change your actions appropriately to ensure that you hit the goal. A perfect example is my trusty diary. I write in it everything I need to for the day. It stays open in my kitchen/living area where I walk past it and look at it tens of times a day. If something is written down, then I do everything in my power to ensure I get it done. If it's not in my diary, there's no way I'm even thinking about it, let alone working towards achieving it. I also get a feeling of satisfaction whenever I complete a task and cross it out. It makes me feel useful and that I have accomplished something that day.

Another big benefit of a written Learning Checklist is that it works with your sub-conscious mind. It is like a program for your sub-conscious mind to help you achieve the goal you have set. It keeps your focused and without really thinking about it you will find yourself working towards it. It becomes a written contract to yourself, which usually sparks a personal motivation to achieve the goal. So basically it makes us accountable to ourselves that we need to accomplish the set tasks everyday.

What time during the day should I implement the Program with my child?

It is a well known fact that morning is the best time for learning, for anyone, at any age. This is because the body wakes up refreshed, ready for the day. This is also the reason why schools usually spend the first morning session teaching the core subjects English and maths, before recess, as they know that the child is more attentive and focussed in the morning. Have you also considered why sports and creative arts are taught in the last session of the school day? This is usually when the child is exhausted from a long day of learning and play at recess and lunch. So how much effort and focus will they put into the activities set for the last session of the day? This reflects the school's perspectives about the importance of sports and creative arts subjects as compared to English and maths.

The same applies with a young child. The morning is the best time when she is refreshed from sleep. Choose a time after your child has eaten and not in a wingy mood. You can let her play a bit before you start the Program, but it is better to for your child to see that play is the reward or incentive she gets when she finishes her 'learning' each day. So in the morning after breakfast is the best time for learning.

If you have younger children at home, such as toddlers or babies that may get in the way when you teach your child, then it would make sense to teach your child when the baby is having her day nap. That way, there are no distractions and you have no excuse for not completing the activities. From previous experience and knowledge, busy mothers usually use their baby's nap time as an opportunity to catch up on all the housework they couldn't do when the baby is awake. However, it is important to accept the common saying, *housework never ends!* Prioritising is the key, and assuming your baby naps an average of 2 hours at a time (and many babies sleep for even longer than that), then first spending 30 minutes of that time teaching your child, and the rest of the nap time doing your other household chores, is a sure way to ensure you do not compromise on your child's learning.

If you have other commitments and find that mornings do not work for you, then experiment with other times of the day and see how you go. Nights are not recommended, as you will be exhausted from your day, and your child will want to wind down and not feel like studying too.

How Much Time Do I Need To Dedicate to the Program?

It is recommended that you dedicate at least 3-4 sessions a week to teaching the Program. Each session should be at least 30 minutes each. Having said this, you will see that all the Checklists (except Checklist 1) include more than one section. So how much time do you allocate for each section in the Checklist? It is not the purpose of this Program to make it hard to implement or be so rigid that it turns the parent off. There is no need to time each section of the Checklist. This is because each section will take different amounts of time to implement. For example, one section of Checklist 2 involves the child identifying her name on a paper. This section will take less than 10 seconds. However, the section that follows it, which involves revising alphabet sounds using the Starfall website, may take 6-10 minutes. Work through each section of the Checklist and keep track of the time. The aim is to finish all the sections of the Checklist within 30 minutes; but if you want to go a little over that time, that's fine.

Time Allocation for Each Part of the Checklists

Below is an example to show you how many minutes to allocate to each section of Checklist 2. Note, however, that it is only a guide and you can adjust it if necessary. When you reach the other Checklists, you will have developed the knowledge and expertise to determine how long is necessary to cover each section of the Checklist well.

Learning Checklist 2

Day: _____   Date: _____

1 MINUTE	Identify Name	
8 MINUTES	Alphabet Focus: (list letters)	
2 MINUTES	Blend focus: _____ + Starfall blend activity	
5 MINUTES	Write blend words: _____ _____ _____ _____	
10 MINUTES	Raz Kids Online books level:	
4 MINUTES	Daily Writing/tracing (lines, spirals, shapes, alphabet, numbers, objects)	

If you have more time and wish to do more than 3-4 sessions each week, the more the better. The days that you choose do not matter; it is the number of sessions taught that counts. The sessions can be on consecutive or non-consecutive days; it does not matter either. Weekends can also be utilised, if you feel you have more time to spend with your child.

If your child is totally new to the concept of pen and paper, or the alphabet at first, then it makes sense to make the teaching sessions less than 30 minutes at first, then gradually increase them over time as your child's attention span and focus increases. But note that Checklist 1 comprises solely of internet activities which your child will love doing, and she will not feel it is learning anyway.

Persevere!

This is one of the most important words emphasised in this book. The longer you persevere with this Program, the more you will see results. It may be difficult at first as you and your child become familiar with each other in this learning situation, but know that you are doing what's best for your child, and your child will thank you later. Many parents feel frustrated being in a teaching position with their child, as they feel they are not 'qualified' to do this; but rest assured that you do not need a teaching degree to teach your child. Just a bit of patience and perseverance.

Reward Your Child's Learning with Incentives

Some mothers feel that they can't or aren't able to teach their child. They say that their child doesn't listen to them, that she just wants to go off and play or do something else. This may be what some mothers feel, but it is not a true indication of the potential of you and your child working together. Most of the time it is because you have not persevered with your child long enough, or you are teaching your child when they are hungry, or tired, or when they usually have their play time. You also may be exhausted and want to rest, and may be communicating this impatience to your child.

Many mothers also feel that their child will not sit down and agree to study, especially at the age of 3 or 4 years. This is completely understandable, however easily overcome. Since children thrive on rewards and incentives—especially to reinforce their behaviour, then it would make sense to reward your child with something she likes at the end of the learning session each day.

Before you begin each teaching session, tell your child that you are going to reward her with something after she completes her learning for the day, so she has something to look forward to. You can also remind your child of the reward while she is learning, if you notice she begins to lose interest during that time. Sometimes, if it is a tangible reward, you can display that reward in front of your child during her learning session, so it can act as a reminder and motivation while she is doing her work. Below is a brief explanation of some types of rewards and incentives and how they can be used to motivate your child and keep her on track while learning.

Sticker chart

Sticker charts can be implemented at the start of the Program to motivate your child during her learning sessions. Your child can receive a sticker at the end of each learning session. Many parents find that letting their child shop for the stickers before the Program and choosing which sticker they want on the chart each day can also keep them more motivated to stick to the Program. When your child reaches the end of the line, she receives a small prize. This can be something as big or small as you want. Some examples of prizes include a fancy pencil, textas, a packet of chips, or anything small you know your child would like. The numbers of boxes in each row will depend on your child's age and how often you think she needs to be rewarded. Usually between 4 and 10 boxes for each row is appropriate, with the number of boxes increasing by age and as maturity increases.

Below are two samples of sticker charts you can implement with your child, rewarding her with a sticker/stamp when she accomplishes her learning goal each learning day. These can found in larger format in the Index, or you can create your own for the Program.

 REWARDS CHART   Name: _____

Monday				
Tuesday				
Wednesday				
Thursday				
Friday				
Saturday				
Sunday				

Image: digitalart / FreeDigitalPhotos.net

LEARNING CHART
Name: _____

Monday	Tuesday	Wednesday	Thursday	Friday	Saturday	Sunday
Monday	Tuesday	Wednesday	Thursday	Friday	Saturday	Sunday
Monday	Tuesday	Wednesday	Thursday	Friday	Saturday	Sunday

Image: digitalart / FreeDigitalPhotos.net

Samples of Rewards charts you can use with your child to motivate her throughout the program

Play time

The fact is: young children's lives involve much play. That's fine, but why not make it a reward for your child instead of a privilege, or something she demands without having to work for? After she learns for the day, she can have some play time, maybe with something she loves, such as painting or play dough. Of course your child will play many times during the day, but reminding your child of play time before learning can act as a reinforcement and motivation during her learning time.

Sweet treat

Sweet treats have been used by mothers for ages to promote and encourage good behaviour and act as a form of reward for achievement. Many children receive at least one sweet treat a day, some without any good reason. If sweet treats are common in your household, then why not let your child work for it? Explain to your child that she will get her sweet when she completes her work today. It is also a good idea to let your child choose the sweet, perhaps from a lolly jar, and place it within view while learning, to act as a constant reminder during the learning time.

Trip to park/outing

If you plan on going on an outing that you know your child will love, such as to the shops, or park, you can tell your child that if she does her work today, you will take her on that outing. It's another way of getting your child to follow instructions without having to organise more trips or pay for extra rewards/incentives.

Computer/Video game

If video games are a part of your child's play time, then having her work for that reward will give her something to look forward to. Many children enjoy video or computer games, and rewarding them with a bit of video game time at the end of their learning can be a way of getting them to do their work.

Now you are mentally prepared for the Program. Now it's time to see the Checklists in action.

Chapter 2

The Resources

The great thing about this Program is that the resources are easily obtained and are at minimal cost to the parent.

Phonics and Sight Words Flashcards—Phonics flash cards can have a letter of the alphabet and corresponding picture printed on the same or opposite side of the flash card. You do not need any expensive or elaborate looking type—just one that does the job. School Zone is a publisher of great quality flash cards at a tiny price—their flash cards sell for $4.95 at many newsagents or educational book suppliers such as Big W, K Mart, Dymocks or Target in Australia.

Alphabet flash cards with letter and picture on same side

Alphabet flash cards with letter and picture on opposite sides

Starfall.com website—This is an amazing free website that plays a major role in the beginning stages of the Program. The website states it is "a free public service to teach children to read with phonics. Our systematic phonics approach, in conjunction with phonemic awareness practice, is perfect for preschool, kindergarten, first grade, second grade, special education, homeschool, and English language development (ELD, ELL, ESL). Starfall is an educational alternative to other entertainment choices for children." What's also great about the website is that it's hand-on and interactive, colourful and fun for little hands to navigate.

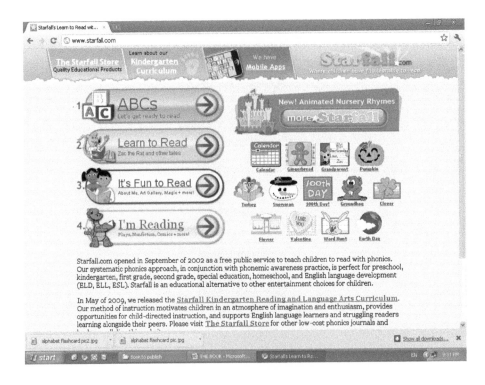

Homepage of Starfall website

Raz-Kids.com website—This website contains hundreds of animated levelled books that children can use to improve their reading. They have the option of listening to books for modelled fluency, then reading the books with pronunciation and vocabulary support. Then they can abandon the "training wheels" and read online books without support. Worksheets or comprehension quizzes are also provided for each each book. What I like about the website is that the online books are interactive,

---

Starfall™ is a registered trademark

with colourful pictures accompanying the text, and some books are accompanied with sound effects. All the books are levelled; starting from absolute beginner until Year 5 reading level. There are on average 20 books for each reading level in the early levels, and over 400 books in total on the website. This makes it an effective resource to use for the whole family, even as kids progress. There is an annual fee of US $79.95 payable for use of the website. However, you can sign up to 36 students when you make an account with them, so your other children or family and friends can also use the website with one annual subscription. This website plays an important role in the Program, but it can be substituted for other resources if desired.

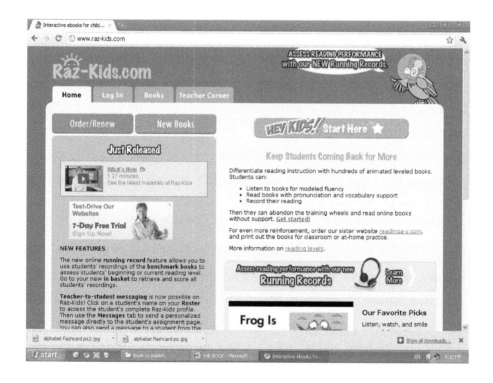

Homepage of Raz-Kids website

Starfall™ is a registered trademark

Library Readers—these are levelled reading books obtained from your local library. The main branch library in a Council is usually the biggest with the largest variety of levelled readers, so it is best to source the books from there. For example, in NSW (Australia), Liverpool City Library is the main branch library of Liverpool Council, and I sourced a lot of levelled books for my daughter from there when implementing the Program with her. There is usually an area in the library dedicated specifically for beginning readers which has the books in crates according to reading level. The library will lend out the books to you for 3 weeks, and you can renew the books up to 2 times after that (if nobody has placed a reservation on the book). This means books can be kept for up to 9 weeks. A useful trick that I learned from university is that you can place a reservation on a book (which can be in any of the library branches) through the library's online catalogue, and then pick them up from your local library when they arrive (you can track the progress of the books online through your library record). This is especially helpful when you don't have time to search through books or go to different library branches to find a specific book. The educational publisher Nelson Cengage Learning offers a wide variety of levelled reading books.

Some of their most popular book series are PM Plus, PM Gems, PM Library and PM Photo Series. The PM Plus series are especially useful and have proven effective to assist a child to read from scratch. These are very popular levelled reading books used in many schools across Australia. The back of the book, or the inside front or back cover will indicate what reading level the book is.

Utilising the reading resources of the library means you don't have to spend hundreds of dollars on reading resources for your child. Usually the child will need to read between 6 and 10 books of the same reading level before she can progress to the next reading level. However, if you don't want to spend time at the library you can opt to purchase the books from the actual publisher itself (contact the publisher or visit their website) or from an educational book supplier in your local area, who can get the books for you if you order through them.

If you want to order the PM Plus levelled reading books from Nelson Cengage Learning (*www.nelsonprimary.com.au*), each book costs AU $7.95. So if you are considering purchasing 6 books from each level 1 – 10, that will be 60 books in total. Reading level 10 is considered a Year 1 level, so having access to levelled reading books up to that reading level will be of great help when your child is reading at a much faster pace as she progresses through the Checklists. The total cost of 60 books at AU $7.95 each is AU $477. Some educational book suppliers may provide a 10-15% discount on their books too, so that can bring down the cost of the books. As mentioned earlier, it is not necessary to purchase the books as you can borrow them from your library, but if you want to invest in the books, maybe to use with your other young children when they are ready to read, the books are a great asset and will save you time searching the libraries for them.

Sight Words—You will need a list of kindergarten sight word which will assist you in teaching your child to memorise the sight words. These can be obtained from a deck of flash cards, or you can make your own. School Zone offers flash cards you can purchase at a small price. These can be sourced from a book supplier or your local retail outlet such as Big W (in Australia).

Sight word flash cards

Sight Words cards are useful in the later stages of the program, so they do not need to be purchased straight away. A list of common sight words is provided in the Index.

Blends words—This consists of common blends such as "at", "in" and "ot". You can make up your own or use the ones in the Index. Words like *cat, fat, rat* and *mat* will teach your child sounding out simple words through rhyming activities.

A Scrap Book—for the purpose of beginning reading and writing, a large A3 scrap book is required. Make sure it has no lines and the pages are not so thin that can rip easily from little hands. It is preferable for the pages to be 110GSM (this refers to the thickness of the page, normal A4 paper is 80GSM). Large retailers such as Big W, Target and K Mart (in Australia) supply large, good quality scrap books, advertised as Visual Arts Diaries for AU $8 - $9. Newsagents supply the same books but at a higher price, so visit your local large retailer first.

A3 and A4 Visual arts diaries you will use for tracing and writing activities

As your child progresses through her learning and her pencil grip improves, you can choose smaller scrap books, and later use normal 8mm ruled exercise books. My daughter was using these before her 4th birthday. This teaches your child to adjust her writing as they develop her fine motor skills.

Chapter 3

The Checklists

SUMMARY OF CHECKLISTS

The Program comprises of 4 simple and easy to follow Checklists that you will follow. Each Checklist (except Checklist 1) comprises of several sections that you will assist your child to complete. Each teaching session should be at least 30 minutes. If your child is not used to sitting still for 30 minutes then you can begin for 10-15 minutes and slowly increase the session duration over time. To move on from one Checklist to the other, you child should have mastered certain skills. The individual chapters that follow will explain each Checklist in detail. Each section of the Checklist will be discussed clearly so you know what to do in the Checklist. It's a good idea to have a copy of the Checklist being explained on hand while you are reading the information in the following chapters, so you can constantly refer to it if necessary. Copies of each Checklist are provided in the chapters that follow as well as in the Index. The following table is a brief summary of each Checklist and what it consists of.

CHECKLIST NAME	MAIN SKILLS LEARNT	DURATION OF USE AND WHEN TO MOVE TO NEXT CHECKLIST
Checklist 1: I Know the Alphabet	• Letter names • Letter sounds	Use Checklist 1 at least 4 times a week. Move to Checklist 2 when the child: • Has memorised all the letter names and sounds, or • Has been using Checklist 1 for 2-3 months and memorised most of the alphabet names and sounds
Checklist 2: I Can Read Simple 3-letter Word Blends	• Identify own name • Sound out simple words • Identify basic sight words • Develop fine motor skills through tracing/writing	Use Checklist 2 at least 3 times a week for 2-3 months. Move to Checklist 3 when the child: • Can identify her name • Continues to develop fine motor skills through tracing/writing • Has mastered all the Starfall alphabet activities with ease • Can sound out some simple 3-letter blend words such as *hat, cat* and *mat* • Is enjoying reading books (either from Raz Kids online or own beginner books)

CHECKLIST NAME	MAIN SKILLS LEARNT	DURATION OF USE AND WHEN TO MOVE TO NEXT CHECKLIST
Checklist 3: I Can Trace My Name and Read Simple Sentences	• Trace own name • Read simple sentences • Tracing alphabet and numbers • Identify and read blend words easily	Use Checklist 3 at least 3 times a week for 2-3 months. Move to Checklist 4 when the child: • Can trace name with ease and getting faster at it • Complete Starfall blend activities with ease • Recall some basic sight words in a text
Checklist 4: I Can Read Sight Words and Sentences	• Write name on her own • Read longer sentences • Progress to more reading levels on Raz Kids or from library books • Sound out and write 3-letetr blend words • Introduce new sight words	• Use Checklist 4 for at least 3 times a week until needed. • Continue for as long as possible. The more you implement the teaching sessions, the more your child will progress.

Checklist 1:
I Know The Alphabet

The first part of the Program consists of teaching your child the alphabet and the sound each letter makes. Checklist 1 requires you to commit to at least 30 minutes a day to the activities, at least 4 times a week.

A child may be familiar with some alphabet letters if you have previously spent time with her with flashcards or an alphabet book. However it is not necessary for the child to have any previous knowledge of the alphabet before starting the Program.

Resources to use for Checklist 1

- Starfall.com website
- An alphabet book (optional)
- Alphabet flash cards (optional)

To implement Checklist 1 you will need the Internet to access the website, www.starfall.com. It teaches the alphabet letters and sounds in a fun interactive way and the child enjoys the process of learning as she is navigating through the website. If you are not sure about the sound a letter makes (and some people are not sure, as they know the letter name but get confused with the sound it makes, even adults!), then you should have a practise run of the Starfall website on your own, and listen to how the activities pronounce the sound when they are introducing each letter at the beginning.

Alternatively, there are numerous videos online showing the alphabet sounds. Check these ones out from You Tube, which will assist you to ensure you know and can teach your child the correct sound each letter makes. (The first one is a no-nonsense one which goes through the sounds in a straight-forward way. The second one incorporates music and is in the form of a song even the child may enjoy.)

http://www.youtube.com/watch?v=vXsmyzjX6_E
http://www.youtube.com/watch?v=saF3-f0XWAY&feature=related

Initially, you will need to assist your child navigate through the website but as she gains confidence, you need only monitor her as she takes part in the alphabet activities. On the following page is the first Checklist you will be using. It comprises of 2 sets of the alphabet.

Checklist 1 for Alphabet Sounds

Day: _____ Date: _____

Circle letter sounds focused on today

a   b   c   d   e   f   g

h   i   j   k   l   m   n

o   p   q   r   s   t   u

v   w   x   y   z

Circle letters child can identify sound off by heart

a   b   c   d   e   f   g

h   i   j   k   l   m   n

o   p   q   r   s   t   u

v   w   x   y   z

Checklist 1 comprises of a few simple yet important text which will be the driving motivation and encouragement you need to keep going in the Program. On the top you will need to fill in the day of the week as well as the date in short form, such as 28/2. Keeping a record of the date of each session will help you monitor how long it takes for your child to progress through the first Checklist. Also, writing down the day of the week will keep you motivated to complete the activities on most days of the week; otherwise you will feel a sense of guilt if there are more than a few days gap between the days you implemented the Checklist.

The alphabet at the top of Checklist 1 is there for you to choose a few letters as the focus for the activities for the day. Let's say you choose the letters *k, m, o* and *x*. Circle those letters on the top alphabet. Now turn your child's attention to the Starfall website, go to the icon **ABCs Lets Get Ready to Read**, and play the activities corresponding with those letters on the website. Lower and upper case letters are introduced in each activity. The activities corresponding with each letter take between 1 and 3 minutes to complete each. Initially, your child may take a little longer as she becomes familiar with the computer skills required for the activities on the website. Some letter activities comprise of a revision component too, which will assist the child to practise and revise some letters, as well as introduce her to lower and upper case letters. The shiny recurring stars throughout the activities indicate that your child needs to click onto them into order to progress through the activities.

Speak to your child as she plays the activities and ask questions throughout, to assist her in revising the letter being learnt.

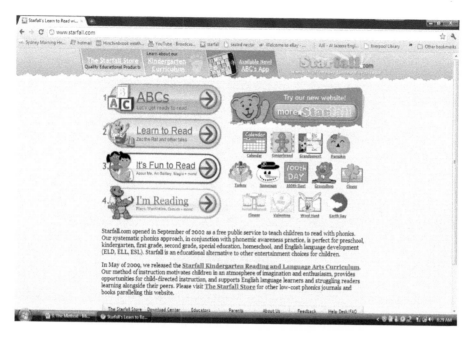

The home website of www.Starfall.com

The list of letters shown after clicking on to ABCs, let's get ready to read.

Starfall™ is a registered trademark

*A sample activity page from the letter **k** activity page.*

Take notice of the shiny stars on the letter k bottom right, indicating to the child she needs to click onto it so the activity can progress.

Starfall™ is a registered trademark

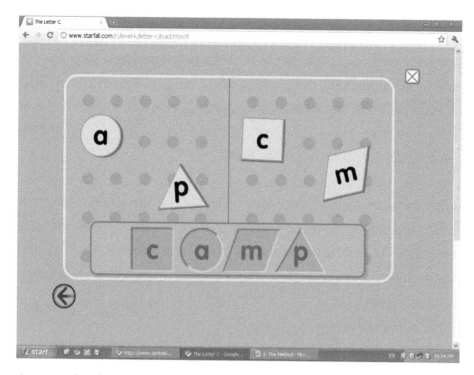

An example of revision activities part of the letter C to help consolidate letter sounds.

The alphabet at the bottom you will use to assess the child at the end of the Starfall session. The purpose is to determine what your child knows of the letter sounds. You can use a set of alphabet flashcards (such as those mentioned earlier from School Zone) or use an alphabet book, or just point to the alphabet letters printed onto the bottom of Checklist 1. Point to one letter at a time (the letters need to be read out randomly, not in order). Ask the child what sound each letter makes. If she knows the sound, then place a tick above the letter.

When assessing your child, focus on the actual letter sound, not the letter name. For example, when asking the child what sound the letter *f* makes,

Starfall™ is a registered trademark

she needs to say *'ffff'*, not *'ef'*. Obviously after the first Checklist you complete with your child, she may not know any alphabet sounds off by heart. Not surprisingly, though, many children may have some knowledge of letter names or sounds that you may not be aware of, as they may have picked up from being with their older siblings or shared reading book experiences they have had in the past.

After you have assessed your child on all the alphabet letters, and placed ticks accordingly, count the number of ticks you have made and write the number in a circle on the right of the bottom alphabet. This will give you a quick indication of the number of letter sounds your child knows up to this time.

Below is an example of what an initial Checklist 1 may look like.

Checklist 1 for Alphabet Sounds

Day: _Tuesday_   Date: _24/2_

Circle letter sounds focused on today

(a) (b) c d e (f) g

h i j k l (m) n

o p q (r) s t u

v w x y z

Circle letters child can identify sound off by heart

ă b c d e f g

h i j k l m̆ n   (3)

o p q r s̆ t u

v w x y z

The next day, you may like to choose a 1 or 2 new letters the child has not encountered before, as well as a 2 or 3 of the letters from the previous lesson. Do not focus on more than 2 new letters a day. This makes a total of 4 or 5 letters day, some new and some old. It is recommended that your child repeat activities for chosen letters each day, to assist her in revising and consolidating her knowledge of letter names and sounds. After the second day's activities on the Starfall website, assess your child again for the letter sounds she knows using a set of flashcards, or you can point to the letters randomly from any place that has the letters written, such as the actual Checklist 1. Place a tick on top of the letters the child can identify the sounds of. Then on the right of the bottom set of alphabet, write the number of letters your child can identify the letter sounds of, and circle. This will help you monitor your child's progress throughout the duration of the Program.

Of course, the child may or may not have memorised any letter sounds after day 2. That's OK, you are not expecting miracles just yet.

On the following pages are 10 real sample pages of Checklist 1, suggesting the number of letters to focus on, and how a child may progress through the Checklist.

Checklist 1 for Alphabet Sounds

Day: _Monday_   Date: _1/3_

Circle letter sounds focused on today

a (b) c d (e) f g

h i j k l (m) n

o p q r (s)(t) u

v w x y z

Circle letters child can identify sound off by heart

a b c d e f g

h i j k l m n   (l)

o p q r s t u

v w x y z

Checklist 1 for Alphabet Sounds

Day: _Tuesday_   Date: _2/3_

Circle letter sounds focused on today

a (b) c d e f g

h (i) j k l (m) n

o p q (r) (s) t u

v w x y z

Circle letters child can identify sound off by heart

a b̌ c d e f g

h i j k l m̌ n   (2)

o p q r s t u

v w x y z

Checklist 1 for Alphabet Sounds

Day: _Thursday_   Date: _4/3_

Circle letter sounds focused on today

a   b   c   d   e   f   g

h   (i)   j   k   l   (m)   n

o   p   q   (r)   s   t   u

(v)   w   x   y   (z)

Circle letters child can identify sound off by heart

a   b✓   c   d   e   f   g

h   i✓   j   k   l   m✓   n   (4)

o   p   q   r✓   s   t   u

v   w   x   y   z

Checklist 1 for Alphabet Sounds

Day: _Saturday_   Date: _6/3_

Circle letter sounds focused on today

a (b) c d e (f) g

h i j k l m n

o p q (r s) t (u)

v w x y z

Circle letters child can identify sound off by heart

a b c d e f g

h i j k l m n   (4)

o p q r s t u

v w x y z

Checklist 1 for Alphabet Sounds

Day: _Monday_   Date: _8/3_

Circle letter sounds focused on today

a b c d e (f) g

h i (j) k l m n

(o) p q r s t u

(v) w (x) y z

Circle letters child can identify sound off by heart

a b✓ c d e f✓ g

h i✓ j k l m✓ n (6)

o p q r✓ s✓ t u

v w x y z

Checklist 1 for Alphabet Sounds

Day: _Wednesday_   Date: _10/3_

Circle letter sounds focused on today

a (b) c d e f g

h i j k l m n

o p q r (s) t u

(v) w (x) y z

Circle letters child can identify sound off by heart

a ✓b c d e ✓f g

h ✓i j k l ✓m n   (6)

o p q ✓r s t u

✓v w x y z

60

Checklist 1 for Alphabet Sounds

Day: _Thursday_   Date: _11/3_

Circle letter sounds focused on today

(a) b c d e (f) g

h i (j) k l m n

(o) p q r s t u

v w (x) y (z)

Circle letters child can identify sound off by heart

a b c d e f g

h i j k l m n (7)

o p q r s t u

v w x y z

Checklist 1 for Alphabet Sounds

Day: _Friday_   Date: _12/3_

Circle letter sounds focused on today

(a) b (c) d e f g

h i (j) k l m (n)

o p q r s t u

v w (x) y (z)

Circle letters child can identify sound off by heart

a b✓ c d e f✓ g

h i✓ j✓ k l m✓ n

o p q r✓ s✓ t u (q)

v✓ w x y✓ z

Checklist 1 for Alphabet Sounds

Day: _Monday_   Date: _15/3_

Circle letter sounds focused on today

a (b) c d e f (g)

h (i) j (k) l m n

(o) p q r s t u

v w x y (z)

Circle letters child can identify sound off by heart

a b✓ c d e f✓ g

h i✓ j✓ k l m✓ n

o p q r✓ s✓ t u   (9)

v✓ w x✓ y z

Checklist 1 for Alphabet Sounds

Day: _Wednesday_   Date: _17/3_

Circle letter sounds focused on today

a b (c) (d) (e) f g

h i j k l m n

(o) p q r s (t) (u)

v w x y z

Circle letters child can identify sound off by heart

a b̌ c d e f̌ g

h ǐ ǰ k l m̌ n

ǒ p q ř š t u   (10)

v̌ w x̌ y z

If you have been using Checklist 2-3 months, and your child still hasn't memorised all of the letter sounds, but most of them, then it is time to move on to Checklist 2. A child does not need to know the entire alphabet sounds to start reading words, and the letters she does not know yet you will continue to focus on them throughout Checklist 2.

Checklist 2:
I Can Read Simple
3-Letter Blend Words

Checklist 2 is the next step you will take with your child when she has successfully memorised all of the letter names, or most of them. It is an exciting stage, one where you introduce important and fundamental reading and writing skills that will set your child up for life. Checklist 2, and the rest of the Checklists after that, comprise of a series of parts that you will assist your child to complete each teaching session. Each time your child accomplishes each part, you place a tick next to the corresponding part. This helps to motivate you to stick to the Checklist.

Use Checklist 2 for at least 3 times a week, with each session comprising of around 30 minutes. The session can be longer if you and the child desire. Continue Checklist 2 for 2-3 months.

Resources to use for Checklist 2

- A3 Visual Arts Diary (such as Derwent brand from Big W)
- Highlighter
- Pencils, textas, pens
- Starfall website
- Raz-kids online books website

What your child will learn in Checklist 2

- Identifying her name
- Revising letter sounds
- Reading and sounding out blends (e.g. fat, rat, mat)
- Identifying some sight words
- Writing and tracing letters and pictures for fine motor skills

On the following page is what Checklist 2 looks like.

Learning Checklist 2

Day: _____   Date: _____

Identify Name	
Alphabet Focus: (list letters)	
Blend focus: _____ + Starfall blend activity	
Write blend words: _____ _____ _____ _____	
Raz Kids Online books level:	
Daily Writing/tracing (lines, spirals, shapes, alphabet, numbers, objects)	

Below is a filled-in sample after Day 1 of completing the Checklist 2 activities.

Learning Checklist 2

Day: _____ Date: _____

Identify Name *Halima*	
Alphabet Focus: *h, j u*	
Blend focus: *a t* + Starfall blend activity	
Write blend words: *mat* *cat* *fat* *rat*	
Raz Kids Online books level *aa*	
Daily Writing/tracing (lines, spirals, shapes, alphabet, numbers, objects)	

Identifying her name

It is important for a child to be able to recognise her name by sight. Identifying and writing her name is an important skill for your child, and one she will be using in the first year of her school life. The more she is exposed to seeing her name the more can memorise its shape and identify it as her own name. Many children enter Kindergarten not being able to write their name, despite attending Preschool. This can make school life more difficult for the child to adjust to, as she will be expected to write her name on many of her work in class.

Start Checklist 2 by writing the child's name on the actual Checklist (as shown in the Checklist on the previous page), or write her name in the Visual Arts diary in large size. Then, point to the child's name and tell her it is her name. After a few days with the Checklist you can ask your child *What does this word say*? And she will learn to reply that it is her name. This form of repetition by starting the Checklist everyday with her name will gradually assist her to memorise her name—its shape and the letters that it consists of.

Revising alphabet sounds

In Checklist 1 your child was introduced to the alphabet letters and their sounds. However, just as anything worth learning, if she does not revise what she has been taught, she will forget them. So Checklist 2 will involve your child spending a little bit of time on a few of the alphabet letter activities from the Starfall website. It is wise to focus on the letters your child is having trouble memorising from the previous Checklist, if that is the case. Each day you will choose at least 3 letters you want your child to revise by doing the Starfall activities. You may want to choose a few different letters each day, and may repeat the same letter for a few days to consolidate her learning. For example, you may choose the letters **h, j** and **u** on one day, then the letters **p, u** and **y** the following day, then the letters **p, j, l** and **s** the next day. It is not necessary to follow the letters in any order or even to stick to the same number of letters each day. You can let your child dictate what letters she wants to choose each day, as long as she is revising alphabet letters and their sounds so that she does not forget them.

Introducing blends

In this part of the Checklist you will introduce to your child 2 letters blended together to make one sound, a 'blend'. One example is *at*, as in *cat, rat, mat*, etc. The purpose of this is to teach your child that different words can make the same blends sound. This will teach your child to blend the first letter with the blend to make some short words she will eventually sound out and read on her own.

The Starfall website contains excellent activities for this part of the Checklist. On the homepage of the Starfall website, click onto *Learn to Read*. Here you will reach the page that contains all of the blends activities. For use in this Program, only the first nine blends are used, as these are the ones suitable for the child's level. These blends are **an, at, en, et, ig, ip, ot, og** and **ug**.

After clicking on to *Learn to read* on the Starfall home page, this is the page that will appear.

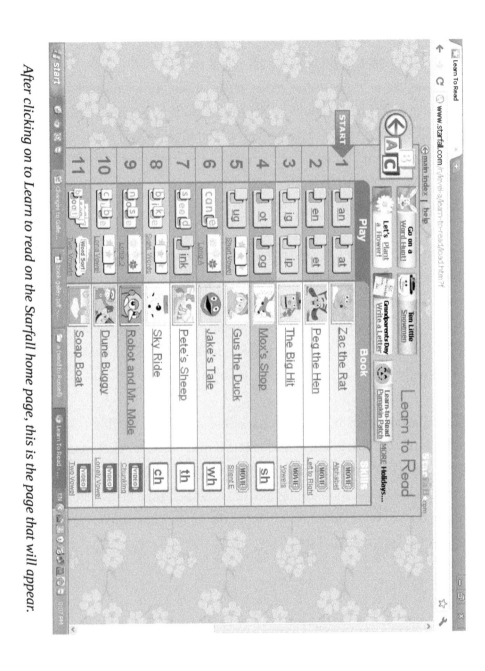

Starfall™ is a registered trademark

Each day, choose a blend (from the first nine mentioned) to focus on and play the activities. At first, you will assist your child with the activities in each blend by repeating the instructions (if necessary) and the actual word by focusing on the initial first sound of the word. You may need to stretch the word so that your child can hear the first letter of the word. For example, for the word (rat), you may need to say (rrrrrrat) so that your child can hear the first letter of the word and complete the activity. Your child will quickly master this skill over a few days.

For example, you may choose the **an** blend the first day, the **at** blend the following day, and the **ot** blend the third day. It is not necessary to do the blends in any particular order. But repetition is a must. Every 2 or 3 days, repeat a blend that you have played before. This will assist your child to consolidate her blending skills and to revise what she has learnt.

*An activity from the **at** blend. Your child will need to drag a letter from the left to match the initial sound of the blend which will make the word as indicated from the picture.*

Writing blend words

The next part of Checklist 2 will involve your child consolidating the skills learnt from the previous blends activity in the Starfall blend. She will attempt to break down and spell the letters required to form basic 3-letter words from the blend activity she has just completed.

For example, if on a particular day you have focused on the *at* blend, then the corresponding words introduced in the Starfall blend activity will be *fat, cat, rat* and *bat*. These are the words you will focus on that day. Write them down on the Checklist.

Using the A3 visual arts diary, ask your child how does she write the word *cat*. Say the word, then break it up so your child can hear the letters clearly. For example, say *cat*, then *c—a—t*. As your child attempts to say the letters, write the correct letter down in large size in the A3 diary, using a bright coloured highlighter, then repeat the word. Then move on to the next word, such as *fat*, and do the same thing. Write each word underneath the previous, so that the child can see the familiar pattern in each of the words in the blend. You do not need to do this part of the Checklist on paper each day. You can alternate to make the activity more fun, by using different materials. Other suggestions are:

- **Using Microsoft Word:** open up a blank document and, using large font size and a bright colour, do the activity on the computer.
- **Using a Doodle Pro:** or any other similar writing toy, you can do the activity using the magnetic pen (see below)
- **Using texta or paint on a large piece of paper**

The aim of this activity is to help your child sound out the words, in a fun and interactive environment.

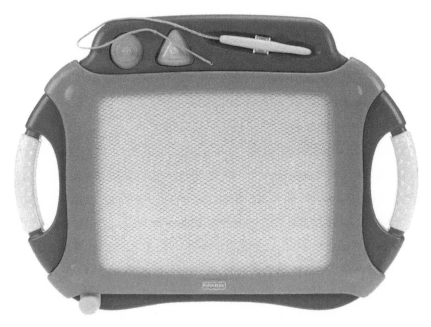

Your child can use her Doodle Pro or something similar to write the blend words. This makes it more fun as she is experimenting with different writing tools.

Daily tracing/writing

One of the best things you can give your child in life is a pencil. Learning to write is one of the first steps your child will take in embarking on her academic life. Activities that help her trace, write letters, learn shapes, and hold a pencil will give your child added practice in learning how to write.

Each day you will build your child's confidence in writing by letting her trace simple lines and shapes, and then proceeding to letters.

These skills begin by simply providing your child with the chance to use different writing materials such as crayons, textas and pencils. She needs to feel the writing tool in her hand and work with it in order t;o reach a good comfort level, as well as practice holding it correctly.

Your child needs to be given the opportunity to just have fun with it at first. Free style art and drawing, drawing a house, a dog, mum, the moon . . . anything you can think of. This will allow her brain to begin making the connection from mental imaging to hand motion.

Allowing your child to learn the fine motor skills of top to bottom, left to right, and circular or curved motion is also essential for pre-writing.

So at first, you need to give your child the opportunity to hold a pencil and trace and draw.

A hi-lighter is a great tool at this stage. It creates a bright line the child can follow, and allows the child some leeway when tracing over the line as it will be thick.

Every day, draw some of the following with a hi-lighter in large size and have your child trace over them:

- Different types of lines such as zig-zag, curved and straight
- Simple shapes such as squares and circles, later progressing on to stars, ovals and heart shapes
- Basic drawings of everyday things such as the sun, tree, people, house, flower
- The child's hand
- Alphabet letters in large size
- Numbers 1-10
- Simple animals shapes such as those of a snake, butterfly
- Spirals

At first, your child's handwriting will be messy. She will not be tracing neatly and will go out of the lines. Don't worry. That's the way each child begins. But it is the consistency that will pay off. No child is born a writer. And the only way to develop her fine motor skills is with practice, practice and more practice! It does not matter what your child draws or traces. Or what writing tool she uses to trace with. It's the opportunity to do it that matters.

How much writing practice each day? Start with one A3 page a day and eventually progress to two. Remember the work she will be tracing will be in large size so not much will fit on to one page.

Below are samples of work completed by a 3-year old child, involving lines drawn using a high-lighter or thick texta, and the child tracing over them to help with fine motor skills.

Zig zag lines

Experimenting with open and closed shapes

Drawing images of familiar objects and family members

Familiar objects and introducing line patterns

Tracing around your hand or the child's can be a fun way for your child to learn about curved lines

More familiar objects

Drawing borders can teach your child about continuous lines, and tracing letters or isolated numbers can be introduced if your child is ready at this stage

Spirals and snakes can be fun to trace!

Tracing over common shapes and hearts also help with shape identification

A child will enjoy tracing over a familiar scene from her memory

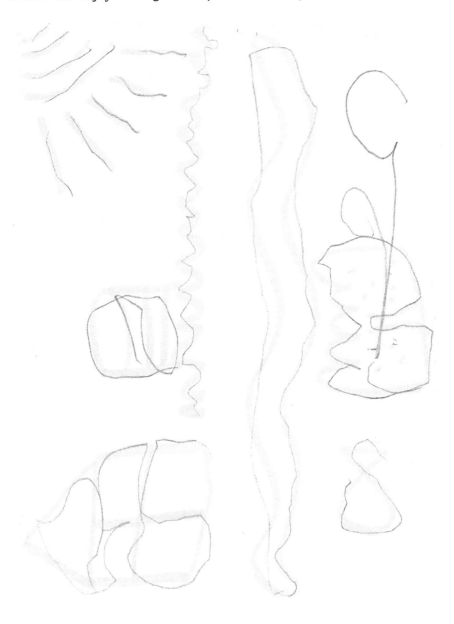

Over time you will notice your child's tracing will be more defined

If you prefer that your child trace over worksheets printed from the internet or book, you can use them instead of hand written worksheets. However, they may not necessarily do a better job than the lines and drawings you write by hand. Also, there is the added issue of ensuring you have internet access and a printer to print the worksheets. If you still prefer internet worksheets, or want to use a combination of both hand-written and internet worksheets, check out these sample worksheets on the following pages. In addition, the Index provides some useful websites with ready-to-print tracing worksheets.

SAMPLE TRACING PAGES

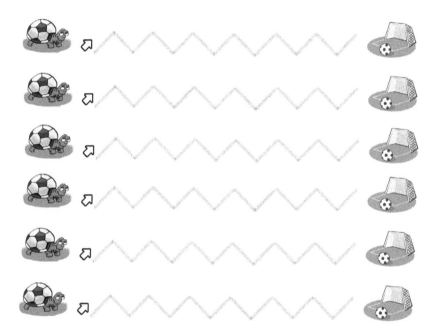

(worksheets copyright of JustMommies.com, reprinted with permission from JustMommies.com)

Trace the rays around the smiling sun and then color the beautiful sun

How many points of sunshine rays can you count?

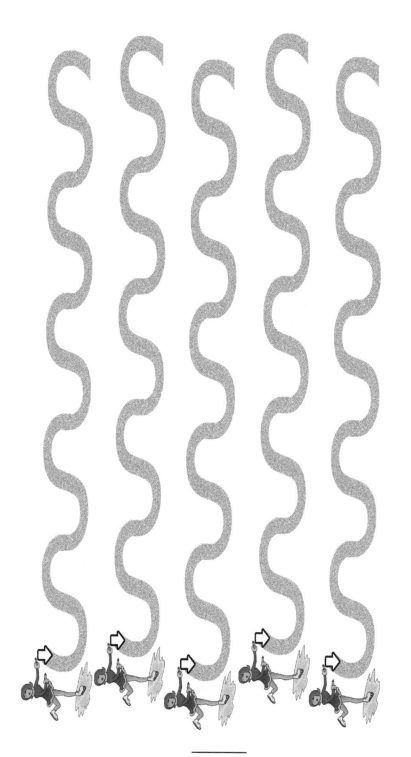

Trace the flower petals and leaves then color the beautiful flower

(worksheets copyright and reprinted with permission from Printactivities.com)

(worksheets copyright and reprinted with permission from Printactivities.com)

GHEDA ISMAIL

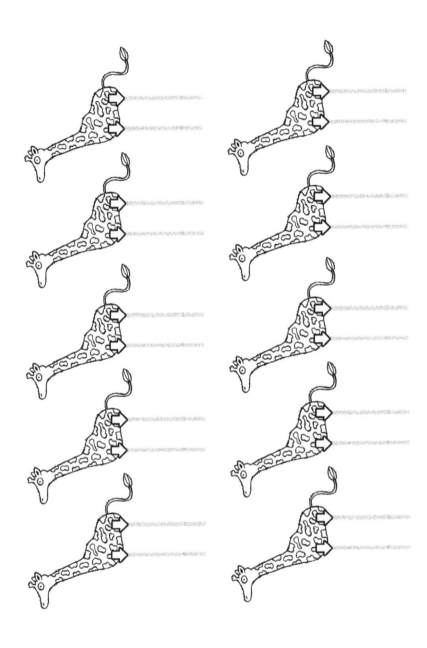

(worksheets copyright of JustMommies.com, reprinted with permission from JustMommies.com)

(worksheets copyright and reprinted with permission from
Printactivities.com)

(worksheets copyright and reprinted with permission from
Printactivities.com)

Instructions: trace and then copy letters or words

Aa Aa Aa Aa

Aa Aa Aa Aa

Ava ate an apple.

BICYCLE

BIRD

BED

BELL

(worksheets copyright and reprinted with permission from
Printactivities.com)

Instructions: trace and then copy letters or words

o o o o

o o o o

look opens a book

Worksheets provided by JustMommies.com

(worksheets copyright of JustMommies.com, reprinted with permission from JustMommies.com)

Raz-Kids Online Reading

To introduce your child to the wonderful world of reading and books the Raz-Kids website has been incorporated into the Program from Checklist 2 onwards. The website consists of books from beginning reading level and progresses to Year 5 level. So it's a great place to gain access to a large amount of reading books all at the same reading level. The books start from level *aa*, which is a preschool level. Level *aa* introduces basic sight words and simple text, in a fun interactive book format. The pictures assist the child to gain meaning from the text.

Every day, choose 2-3 books from the *aa* level to introduce to your child basic sight words. At first, the listening component of the books (indicated by the ear symbol) will be a great tool to start with, as the child will listen to the book being read and hear the correct pronunciation of the words. The interactive pictures and sound effects will add to the appeal of the books for your child. Then, after listening to the book being read, you can assist your child to read the book.

The next day, you can choose a book from the previous day and another one or two new books from the same reading level, **aa**.

The purpose of the Raz-Kids website at first is to expose your child to the world of words and books in a fun atmosphere, in addition to seeing new simple words. Later on your child will learn to identify the words in these texts, and either say them off by heart (from memorising them as they are sight words) or sound them out (as they have been learning to sound out blends in Checklist 2).

If you have access to beginning reading books; either from the local library, or if you have decided to purchase some levelled reading books starting from level 1, then you can also introduce these to your child alongside or in place of the Raz-Kids books.

Below you will find 8 pages of Checklist 2, suggesting the sequence of activities and blends to be focused on over 8 teaching days. But remember it is a suggestion only, and you can choose the blends and letters that you want, as they will all teach fundamental skills.

Learning Checklist 2

Day: _Sunday_   Date: _14/3_

Identify Name *Halima*		✓
Alphabet Focus: (list letters) *h j u*		✓
Blend focus: *at* + Starfall blend activity		✓
Write blend words: *cat mat fat hat*		✓
Raz Kids Online books level: *aa*		✓
Daily Writing/tracing (lines, spirals, shapes, alphabet, numbers, objects)		✓

Learning Checklist 2

Day: _Monday_   Date: _15/3_

Identify Name Halima	✓
Alphabet Focus: (list letters) p u y v q	✓
Blend focus: ___an___ + Starfall blend activity	✓
Write blend words: ran pan fan can	✓
Raz Kids Online books level: aa	✓
Daily Writing/tracing (lines, spirals, shapes, alphabet, numbers, objects)	✓

Learning Checklist 2

Day: _Wednesday_   Date: _17/3_

Identify Name *Halima*	✓
Alphabet Focus: (list letters) *p j g c m w*	✓
Blend focus: ___*ig*___ + Starfall blend activity	✓
Write blend words: *big* *wig* *dig* *fig*	✓
Raz Kids Online books level: *aa*	✓
Daily Writing/tracing (lines, spirals, shapes, alphabet, numbers, objects)	✓

Learning Checklist 2

Day: _Friday_   Date: _19/3_

Identify Name	_Halima_	✓
Alphabet Focus: (list letters)	_q g_	✓
Blend focus: _ot_ + Starfall blend activity		✓
Write blend words: _dot cot hot pot_		✓
Raz Kids Online books level: _aa_		✓
Daily Writing/tracing (lines, spirals, shapes, alphabet, numbers, objects)		

Learning Checklist 2

Day: _Monday_   Date: _22/3_

Identify Name _Halima_	✓
Alphabet Focus: (list letters) _q d l_	✓
Blend focus: _og_ + Starfall blend activity	✓
Write blend words: _log frog dog fog_	✓
Raz Kids Online books level: _a a_	✓
Daily Writing/tracing (lines, spirals, shapes, alphabet, numbers, objects)	✓

Learning Checklist 2

Day: _Tuesday_   Date: _23/3_

Identify Name Halima	✓
Alphabet Focus: (list letters) f n c h	✓
Blend focus: _ug_ + Starfall blend activity	✓
Write blend words: _rug_ _bug_ _mug_ _hug_	✓
Raz Kids Online books level: q	✓
Daily Writing/tracing (lines, spirals, shapes, alphabet, numbers, objects)	✓

Learning Checklist 2

Day: _Thursday_   Date: _25/3_

Identify Name Halima		✓
Alphabet Focus: (list letters) k t c		✓
Blend focus: e h + Starfall blend activity		✓
Write blend words: ten pen men hen		✓
Raz Kids Online books level:		
Daily Writing/tracing (lines, spirals, shapes, alphabet, numbers, objects)		✓

Learning Checklist 2

Day: _Friday_   Date: _26/3_

Identify Name	Halima	✓
Alphabet Focus: (list letters)	p l h r d	✓
Blend focus: __at__ + Starfall blend activity		✓
Write blend words: cat rat fat bat		✓
Raz Kids Online books level: a		✓
Daily Writing/tracing (lines, spirals, shapes, alphabet, numbers, objects)		✓

How long to use Checklist 2

If you use Checklist for a good 2-3 months, at least 3 times a week, your child can progress to Checklist 3. Signs your child is ready for Checklist 3 include:

- Your child can identify her name when she sees it
- Your child is developing her fine motor skills and this is evident in her improved ability to trace shapes and lines
- Your child completes the Starfall alphabet activities with ease and it is clear she knows all of the alphabet sounds
- Your child is becoming increasingly confident with the blends activities in the Starfall website and can do them with ease or with minimal assistance
- Your child can hear the sounds in a simple word such as *mug*, and can tell you the letters or sounds that are in each word when you break up the word for her, such as *m—u—g*
- Your child is enjoying the Raz-Kids online books and is growing in confidence in identifying some of the words in the books, either from picture clues or memorising the word

If your child displays most of the above signs, but not all of them, and you have been using Checklist 2 for at least 3 times a week for 3 months, your child can progress to Checklist 3.

Checklist 3:
I Can Trace My Name and Read Simple Sentences

Checklist 3 continues with many important skills learnt in Checklist 2, with a few exciting new additions. In addition to continuing the essential Starfall blends activities, the Raz-Kids online books and daily writing/tracing, your child will be introduced to:

- Tracing her name everyday
- Simple sentences that she will learn to read every day
- More focus on tracing the alphabet letters

Checklist 3 should be used at least 3 times a day, for 2-3 months, with sessions comprising of at least 30 minutes.

Learning Checklist 3

Day: _____ Date: _____

Identify and Trace Name	
Starfall activity blend focus:	
Read and write blend words: _____ _____ _____ _____	
Sentence Reading:	
Raz Kids Online books level: or readers	
Daily Writing/tracing (shapes, objects, letters, numbers, blends words)	

Resources to use for Checklist 3

- A3 Visual Arts Diary (such as Derwent brand from Big W)
- Highlighter
- Pencils, textas, pens
- Starfall website
- Raz-kids online books website
- levelled reading books from the library (if available), or purchased (if desired

Identifying and tracing name

So far your child has been learning to identify her name when she sees it in Checklist 2. In Checklist 3, as her fine motor skills have been improving, she will be learning to trace her name as well. Once your child begins to feel more confident about making the pencil do what she wants it to do, it's time to have her trace her name on dotted or highlighted letters. This assists with the muscle memory of how to move her pencil while writing the letters of her name.

Every day, you will write your child's name in large size using a hi-lighter on the A3 paper, and she will be practice tracing over her name. Over a period of 1-2 months, if done consistently, your child will be able to write her name by memory on her own.

To start with, write your child's name and ask her whose name it is. She will say her name. If not, tell her it is her name. Then ask your child to write over her name using a pencil or pen.

Pay particular attention to how she writes the letters. Make sure she starts the letters from the correct position. If she learns to write the letters correctly from the start, she will find it easy to write. If your child writes the letters in the wrong way, stop her and show her how to do it. Correction will lead to success.

On the following page is a work sample, showing how a child would trace her name each day.

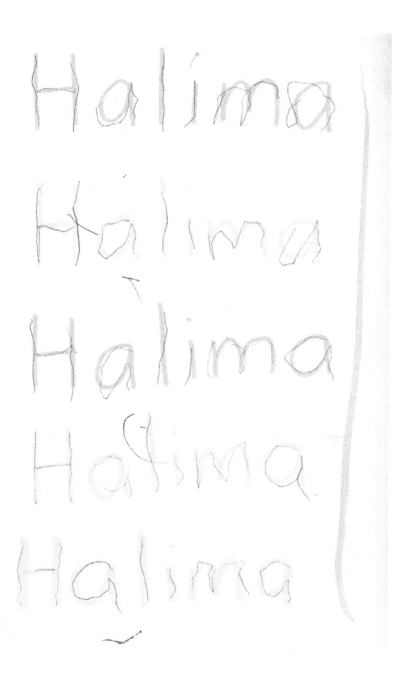

If you prefer that your child traces her name using a proper computer font from a word document, then you can find an appropriate dotted font from the internet and download it. The following is an example of a dotted font which can be downloaded from the internet called National First Font Dotted. If desired, download and extract the font onto your computer, then use it to write your child's name in large size several times on an A4 sheet of paper (as shown below). Your child can then trace her name everyday.

Halima   Awwad

Halima   Awwad

Halima   Awwad

Halima   Awwad

Halima   Awwad

As a general rule, letters always start from the top and go down. Refer to the chart below indicating with arrows the correct way to start writing letters for more detail.

Correct Letter Formation

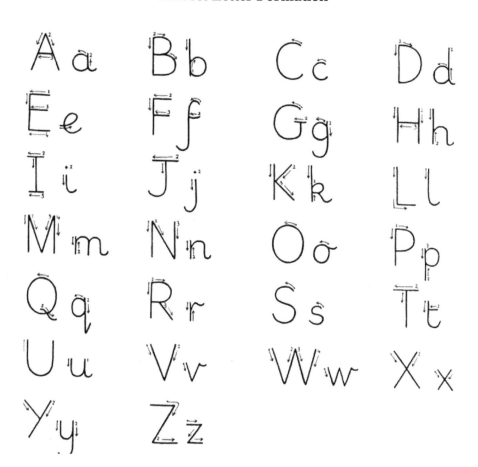

Also pay attention to her pencil grip. Children who begin to hold the pencil the wrong way will be putting extra strain and pressure on their fingers when writing; making it harder for them to write correctly. Their handwriting may be messy and awkward, their hands may hurt when writing and it is clear they are putting extra effort into the task of writing. Show your child how to hold a pencil, and correct her immediately if she holds the pencil the wrong way. The most comfortable known pencil grip is the tripod grasp. It involves using the long finger, the thumb and the Index finger to form a tripod to hold the pencil (see below). If your child has established another grasp, she may find using the tripod grasp awkward at first, but with practice she can effectively change her grasp within a few days or weeks.

The tripod pencil grip

You may want to utilise some stationery aids such as pencil grippers (pictured below) to assist your child with her pencil grip.

Blend reading and writing

This part of Checklist 3 involves consolidating your child's skills in blends. Choose one blend a day to focus on, and let your child play the activities in the Starfall website, such as *an.* After she has completed the online activity, continue with writing the blends words that correspond with the chosen blend, such as *can, man, fan* and *ran.* Refer to the *Writing Blends Words* information in Checklist 2 on page 67 as you will continue to do this in Checklist 3.

The only difference now is that your child will now trace the words you have helped her write as well. This will assist in her fine motor skills as well as help her see how rhyming words have the same letters at the end.

Make sure you are writing the words in large size using a hi-lighter, so then your child can trace these words after you. Then let your child try to read these words by herself.

If you feel your child is ready for flash cards, then now is the time to introduce the Blends Words flash cards to her (see Index). These are the blends words she has been practising from the Starfall website, such as *cat, mat, rat* and *hat.* Cut out the flash cards and use these in this section of the Checklist to consolidate her knowledge of blends and rhyming words. Choose the blends words that your child has been focusing on that day.

Raz-Kids Online books/readers

Continue with the Raz-Kids online reading, progressing along the level **aa**. Choose a few books a day. If your child is ready let her try reading the book on her own, without the assistance of the book being read to her. She can look at the pictures for meaning. The next level after **aa** is level **A**, which is similar in content but more words are introduced. You can let your child read a combination of books from both levels if you wish.

In addition to the Raz-Kids online books, or in place of them, your child can start to read some beginner levelled reading books that you have either borrowed from your local library, or purchased from an educational book publisher (as discussed in The Resources chapter). Choose a few books each day, and remember to reread the books the following day to gain mastery of reading skills.

Daily writing/tracing

Continue developing your child's fine motor skills in Checklist 3 with more tracing of shapes, lines and simple pictures. Now that she may be more confident and have better control of her pencil grip, you can also now introduce/consolidate:

- Tracing the letters of the alphabet (be careful to monitor pencil grip and correct letter formation). While it is important to introduce both lower and upper case letters when tracing, focus more on lower case letters as your child will be exposed to these letters more often in reading and writing.
- Tracing the letters from 1-10.
- Tracing the blends words from the Blends writing activity of that day.
- Letters from a language other than English if you would like to introduce your child to a second language.

Below are work samples reflecting the types of tracing and writing that can be done in this Checklist 3.

Tracing over alphabet letters and numbers

Tracing over letters and familiar objects

Tracing over blend words will teach her to see how words are similar (in letters and sound)

Continue with tracing shapes and objects to consolidate fine motor skills

Over time you will notice your child will improve in tracing and her pencil marks will resemble something very realistic

Tracing different blends words and familiar objects

Your child can also experiment with textas and other writing materials in writing and tracing activities

Colouring in shapes can also be a part of the writing and tracing activities

Sentence Reading

The inclusion of sentence reading in this part of the Program will be the turning point in your child's learning. So far your child has mainly been exposed to literacy at the word level. Now she will be exposed to it at the sentence level.

You will start off with simple sentences that comprise of 3-4 words, which include a combination of simple sight words and words she can or will learn to sound out on her own. The sight words at first will also be words she can sound out, such as **am, is, at,** etc. You may initially only focus on one new sentence for a few days. Later on, as your child becomes confident in reading the words, you will add some more basic sentences to the Checklist, comprising of some of the same words in previous sentences but with a few different words added.

The aim of these sentences is to build up your child's sight word vocabulary as well as give her the opportunity to sound out some basic 3-letter words.

Try to choose sentences that have meaning to your child. If your child doesn't have a pet, then don't choose a sentence about pets. Your child will learn the words if they have meaning to her.

After introducing a new sentence the first day, have the child reread the sentence from the previous day as well as the new sentence of the day. If she does not remember, that's fine, reread the sentence for her and the new sentence before she has a go at reading them.

Keep track of the new sentences that you introduce. After choosing your focus sentence for the day, write it down on the Checklist. Then, write it down in large size in the Visual Arts diary. To make it easier to refer to, use the back of the Visual Arts diary for sentence reading. Rules some lines and write each new sentence of the day on a line. That way, when it comes time to reread previous sentences, you can just refer back to the A3 Visual Arts diary.

Sample sentences to start with

I am big

I am good

I am happy

I am a boy/girl

I like to run

I like to play

I like to hop

(Child's name) likes to share

I can run

I can play

I can jump

I can draw

I can run fast

I have a cat/dog

I have a big ball

My baby is little

My cat/dog is big

My hair is long

My house is big

My toy is big

I go to the shop
I go to the park
I go to the party
I go to school
I go to my friend's house
The toy is little
My cat is little
My friend is little
My ball is little
I am little
Look at my toy
Look at the dog
Look at the house
Look at the flower
Look at my book

List of Sight Words introduced in above sentences

am	a	like	my	I	go
to	have	can	is	little	run
the	school	look	at	jump	

Below are 8 sample pages of Checklist 3, indicating an example of the blends focused on, and the introduction of new simple sentences.

Learning Checklist 3

Day: _Wednesday_

Date: _26/5_

Identify and Trace Name	✓
Starfall activity blend focus: _an_	✓
Read and write blend words: _pan man ran can_	✓
Sentence Reading: _I am big._	✓
Raz Kids Online books level: _9_ or readers	✓
Daily Writing/tracing (shapes, objects, letters, numbers, blends words)	✓

Learning Checklist 3

Day: _Thursday_

Date: _27/5_

Identify and Trace Name	✓
Starfall activity blend focus: _ot_	✓
Read and write blend words: _hot_ _cot_ _dot_ _pot_	✓
Sentence Reading: _I am good._	✓
Raz Kids Online books level: _9_ or readers	✓
Daily Writing/tracing (shapes, objects, letters, numbers, blends words)	✓

Learning Checklist 3

Day: _Friday_

Date: _28/5_

Identify and Trace Name	✓
Starfall activity blend focus: _et_	✓
Read and write blend words: _pet net wet jet_	✓
Sentence Reading: _I am a girl._	✓
Raz Kids Online books level: _a_ or readers	✓
Daily Writing/tracing (shapes, objects, letters, numbers, blends words)	✓

Learning Checklist 3

Day: _Monday_

Date: _31 / 5_

Identify and Trace Name	✓
Starfall activity blend focus: i g	✓
Read and write blend words: big dig jig fig	✓
Sentence Reading: I can run.	✓
Raz Kids Online books level: 9 or readers	✓
Daily Writing/tracing (shapes, objects, letters, numbers, blends words)	✓

Learning Checklist 3

Day: *Tuesday*

Date: *1/6*

Identify and Trace Name	✓
Starfall activity blend focus: *ip*	✓
Read and write blend words: *zip rip lip dip*	✓
Sentence Reading: *I can hop.*	✓
Raz Kids Online books level: *9* or readers	✓
Daily Writing/tracing (shapes, objects, letters, numbers, blends words)	✓

Learning Checklist 3

Day: _Thursday_

Date: _3 / 6_

Identify and Trace Name	✓
Starfall activity blend focus: in	✓
Read and write blend words: pin tin bin fin	✓
Sentence Reading: I can jump	✓
Raz Kids Online books level: a or readers	✓
Daily Writing/tracing (shapes, objects, letters, numbers, blends words)	✓

Learning Checklist 3

Day: _Friday_

Date: _4/6_

Identify and Trace Name	✓
Starfall activity blend focus: _it_	✓
Read and write blend words: _bit_ _mit_ _sit_ _fit_	✓
Sentence Reading: _I like to play._	✓
Raz Kids Online books level: _a_ or readers	✓
Daily Writing/tracing (shapes, objects, letters, numbers, blends words)	✓

Learning Checklist 3

Day: _Monday_

Date: _7/6_

Identify and Trace Name	✓
Starfall activity blend focus: _en_	✓
Read and write blend words: _den_ _pen_ _men_ _hen_	✓
Sentence Reading: _Halima likes to share._	✓
Raz Kids Online books level: _9_ or readers	✓
Daily Writing/tracing (shapes, objects, letters, numbers, blends words)	✓

How long to use Checklist 3

If use Checklist for at least 3 times a week, for a period of 2-3 months, your child is ready for Checklist 4. Signs your child is ready for Checklist 4 include:

- She is beginning to trace her name with ease and is even becoming faster at it
- She can complete the Starfall blends activities quickly and it is clear she understands and knows how to read the blends
- She is recalling some basic sight words from the focus sentence for each day, and is able to remember the words in the previous sentences when she reads them.

Checklist 4:
I Can Read Sight Words
and Sentences

There is not a great big difference between Checklist 3 and 4; however the additions are what will push your child to the next level in her quest to learn how to read and write. In Checklist 4 your child will continue to:

- Trace over her name
- Revise blends through the Starfall website
- Develop her fine motor skills through tracing and writing lines and letters
- Focus on a new sentence of the day

The additions of Checklist 4 include:

- Your child will be encouraged to try to write her name by herself.
- A new sentence will be introduced each day, which may be longer in length than previous sentences in Checklist 3.

- Your child will move on to more levels from the Raz-Kids website
- You will utilise books from the local library that are at the beginner readinglevel (if you have not done so previously)
- Your child will try sounding out basic 3-letter words and attempt writing them down.
- Flashcards will be introduced for sight words to help your child develop fluency in sight word reading and memorisation.

Resources to use for Checklist 4

- A3 Visual Arts Diary (such as Derwent brand from Big W)
- Highlighter
- Pencils, textas, pens
- Starfall website
- Raz-kids online books website
- Levelled reading books from library or ones pre-purchased
- Sight word flashcards (optional)
- Sight word list (see Index)
- Blends flash cards (see Index)

Continue Checklist 4 for as long as you want. Because it is the last Checklist, the more you continue with the sessions the more you will see results. Again, 30 minutes a day for at least 3 sessions is recommended; however if you implement it more than three times a week, you will notice better progress. As you continue with the teaching sessions, you can adjust the Checklist according to your child's capabilities.

Learning Checklist 4

Day: _____ Date: _____

Write Name	
Sentence reading and writing:	
Blend focus:	
Raz Kids books/Readers:	
Sight Word focus:	
Writing/tracing (alphabet, numbers, sound out and write blends words, and simple sentences)	

Writing Name

In Checklist 4 your child may be ready to attempt writing her name by herself. If you have followed the previous Checklists consistently then your child should have seen her name written many times and traced it many times as well. Now is the time to see if your child can try to write her name on her own. Continue reminding her about letter formation and pencil grip when she writes. By now her handwriting should be more legible and neater.

Ask your child if she can write her name on her own. Don't force your child; if she says she can't then start writing it in large size for her at first and have her trace it. But the following day your child may tell you she is ready to write it on her own.

Each day you will begin the teaching session by asking your child to write her name on her own. Correct and give clues as needed.

Sentence Reading and Writing

In Checklist 3 your child was introduced to words at the sentence level. This was done through simple repetitive sentences involving one or two simple sight words, and words that easily be broken up and sounded out by the child. In Checklist 4 you will continue developing your child's sentence reading through sentences that are a little longer in length, such as 4-8 words.

Let you and your child jointly choose a sentence that is meaningful to her. It can be based on something she did on the weekend, something she will be doing soon, or even a sentence telling about a topic.

The sentences will comprise of a combination of simple sight words, easy to sound out words, as well as one or two words that are needed to complete the sentence and ensure it makes sense. An example of a sentence like this is:

It is fun to go to the park.

In the above sentence *it, is, to, go* and *the* are sight words, *fun* is a word that can easily be broken up and sounded out, and *park* is a word needed to complete the sentence (based on a theme or a topic previously discussed).

In this way, your child is gaining practice in:

- reading words she can sound out (fun)
- reading words by sight (*it, is, to, go* and *the*) and
- reading words that can partly be sounded out from the start or the end (park).

An excellent way to fast track your child's reading during these reading activities is to also introduce other spelling rules or blends as they are exposed to on a daily basis. For example, in the process of introducing the word *park* to your child, you can briefly mention that the *ar* in the work *park* makes a long *aaar* sound. You may think that your child won't take this aboard during the process of learning, but be surprised. Over time, and, depending on how long you continue with the Program, you will be exposing your child to many opportunities for reading, and other words may come up that incorporate this spelling rule, such as *star, party* and *hard.* Over time, and through exposure to many sentences, your child will develop the spelling strategies.

Another example of a longer sentence introduced in Checklist 4 is:

Mum and I went to the shops.

In the above sentence **and, I, to** and **the** are sight words, **mum** and **went** are words that can easily be broken up and sounded out, and **shops** is a word needed to complete the sentence (based on a theme or a topic previously discussed).

In this way, your child is gaining practice in:

- reading words she can sound out *(mum* and **went)**
- reading words by sight (**and, I, to** and **the**) and
- reading words that can partly be sounded out from the start or the end (shops).

During the process of teaching the child the word **shops,** briefly mention that the **sh** in **shops** makes a certain sound.

Below is a list of sample sentences that can be used, or partly used and adjusted according to your child's life or experiences.

My baby sister is little.
I want to play with my toy.
(name) and (name) are friends.
They play on the swings.
I have fun on the bike.
I jump on the trampoline.
I go up and down.
I ride on the scooter.

We play with my ball.

I like to go to the beach.

I run on the beach.

We dig with my shovel.

I look at my computer.

We are going to eat pizza.

Today (name) and (name) will play together.

I read a book with (name).

(sibling name) goes to school.

I put on my hat outside.

It is very hot today.

Today I saw (name) at the shops.

I like to go to the zoo.

I make cupcakes at home.

(name) came to my house.

(name) is very sick today.

I play with all my friends.

Where are my books?

I find my books in my bag.

This is a big book.

I get a lolly from the box.

(name) and (name) go to the park.

I will see (name) today.

Dad got a puzzle for me.

I trace in my book.

(name) and (name) played outside today.

Dad got me goggles for swimming.

I do my homework everyday.

I helped Dad cut the grass.

I colour with my pencils.

I like to race in the yard.

She went up the slide.

After you assist your child to read the sentence several times, try pointing to a word and ask her what the word says. Another strategy is to ask the child, **Which word in the sentence is [the] ?** and have your child try pointing to the correct word. This will help consolidate her word recognition.

After reading the sentence, write the sentence into a book and have your child trace over the sentence. As she writes the sentence, assist her to make connections with the letters she writes and their sounds by you sounding out the words as she writes them. This will assist with word recognition, breaking up words as well as fine motor skills.

(Variation to advance your child: If you have been doing sentence reading and writing like this for a few weeks, you may feel your child is ready to start writing the simple sentence on her own, with your assistance. Continue choosing a sentence of the day, then instead of writing the sentence for your child and having her trace over it, you can prompt your child to attempt writing the sentence on her own, by sounding out the words that she can, and helping her with the words she can't. Implement this variation if you feel your child is ready for it. Otherwise, continue with sentence reading and your child tracing over the sentence.

Revising Blends

Your child should have become a professional at the Starfall website and using it, now, as a revision of blends rather than a new learning skill. Your child can continue revising the short blends such as *an, ot, en* and *ug* (the first 9, as introduced in order from the top). She may or may not be ready for the long blends activities that follow, such as ***cane, seed,*** etc (see below). See you how she goes and if she is happy at doing a few of the blends activities she has been previously doing each day, that would be sufficient for revision.

Continue revising blends in this section of the Checklist by also having your child read out the blends words from the flash cards. Focus on one set of blends flash cards each day, corresponding with the one you are revising on that day.

The story books on the right side of the web page can also be introduced to consolidate short vowel blends and to encourage a love for reading.

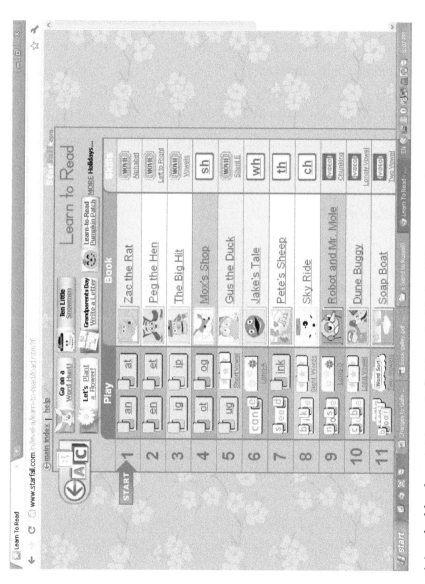

Continue practicing the blends activities as individuated with the START icon on the top left. Continue from [an] until [ug]. The story books on the right side of the web page can also be introduced.

Starfall™ is a registered trademark

After that, choose of the blends such as **an,** and let your child initiate writing the 3-letter blend words in her book. Assist her if necessary by breaking up the word to make the word easier to write. At this stage your child should be learning to sound out a simple 3-letter word on her own. Let her write the four blend words from the activity in her book and practise reading them together.

If your child is still not ready to sound out the 3-letter blend words and write them, then assist your child to sound them out and write them for her, and get her to trace over them.

Raz-Kids Books and Readers

Depending on your child, and how often you are implementing the Program, your child will be progressing through the reading levels of Raz-Kids. It is important not to rush into a new level if your child is not ready. Rather, revision of words in previous books is more important to consolidate learning.

It is not surprising for your child to progress to levels *a, b* and *c* comfortably in the Raz-Kids website. You will feel excited to know that your child is finally beginning to read basic stories! All the hard work has paid off!

To finally reach this stage it is now a real possibility that your child can start to read, with assistance, some leveled reading books from the library.

As previously mentioned in The Resources chapter, PM Plus readers are a great resource you can start utilising with your child. Find out from the main branch of your Council library where they store the beginning reading books, and start flicking through them and choose basic books you think your child can manage to read with assistance. Many books, including the PM Plus books, list the reading level of that book on the back cover, or inside front of inside back cover of the book. Choose levels 1, 2, 3 or whatever you feel your child is ready for. If you are unsure about your child's reading level then the Raz Kids website will list the books' corresponding reading levels as you move the cursor over the desired reading books. Alternatively, or in addition to these books, your child can start reading the levelled reading books that you have purchased, starting from level 1.

The more reading practice, the better. Have your child read for at least 10 minutes a day. Choose a few books from Raz Kids and/or the library books, and assist your child to read them over and over to gain mastery of words. Strategies you can use with your child during reading include:

- Read the title of the book for your child and discuss what she thinks the book will be about
- Read the book for your child slowly, and discuss the pictures
- If your child enjoys the book so much and asks you to reread the book, then do so. Remember the purpose is to develop in your child love of books, not just reading words
- After reading the book to your child, have your child start reading the book
- Encourage your child to look at the pictures to gain meaning and to assist with reading the words that can't be sounded out
- Have your child point to the words as she reads them, or you do this for your child as she reads the words. This will help her make connections with the word and the sounds in it

- If your child comes across a word in the book that you know she has seen before (such as a word from previous sentence writing), encourage her to attempt to read the word
- If you child needs any help, give her minor help by asking her to either sound out the word (if it is a word that can be sounded out like *can*), or ask her to remember how the word sounds (such as *is*) or to look at the picture for clues (if it is a word that can't be sounded out such as *sky*)
- After reading once or twice, stop at a page and ask your child to point to a word you call out (for example, ask you child to point to the word *THE*), or you can point to a word and ask the child to read the word

Above all, make reading time enjoyable and fun by focusing on the topic of the book. If the book is about things in the sky, discuss other things that can be in the sky. This can also lead to brief discussion of weather, which is fine too. Remember your child is also learning new things in the process of reading, so that is a skill in itself.

Sight Word Focus

Even though this section has been added to Checklist 4, your child has already been exposed to sight words (words that cannot be sounded out, but rather memorised from sight only) in previous Checklists through sentence reading and writing and reading books. Now though, is the time to keep a record of the one or two new sight words introduced or revised in sentence reading and writing each day. The purpose of this is to ensure that you do not introduce too many new sight words at one time, and to make sure that previously introduced sight words have been revised and consolidated. Remember, revision of previous sight words is more important that introduction of new ones.

How quickly you progress to new sight words depends on your child's ability to grasp new words and how often you have been implementing the Program. Generally, one or two new sight words are sufficient each week, taking into account a week comprising of at least 3 teaching sessions with your child.

Each teaching session, keep a record in the Checklist of the few sight words that you focus on in the process of reading and writing the new sentence of the day. For example, if the sentence is *I have fun on the slide,* then you will record the sight words you have focused on are *I, have, on* and *the*. At the next teaching session, your new sentence may be *I play on the swings*. This will ensure that the sight words *I, on* and *the* have been revised from the previous day. In addition, *play* has also been introduced in the process of revising previous sight words.

You may feel that your child is ready to use sight word cards to help her revise some of the sight words she is reading everyday. If you think you would like to add this to the teaching session, you can use a deck of sight word cards (such as those mentioned from School Zone) and go through a few of the sight words your child has been exposed to everyday. However it is not necessary if you feel your child is not ready for rote reading of sight words just yet.

There are no hard rules on which sight words to focus on first, and in which order, but a general rule is to focus on the short simple ones first. The following list is a great one to start off with.

SIGHT WORD LIST

a	and	away
big	can	come
down	for	go
here	I	in
is	it	jump
like	little	look
make	me	my
not	on	play
run	said	see
the	to	up
we	where	you

Writing/Tracing

Daily tracing and writing still forms an important part of your child's learning as she continues to master correct pencil grip and letter formation. The more practice she gets in tracing, the more her fine motor skills will develop. At this stage your child will get writing practice when:

- tracing over the blend words, but it is also important to
- practise tracing the alphabet letters and
- numbers 1-10 or 1-20 depending on the child's level

These will also assist her at school when learning about dictionary order (when she can identify the order of the letters) as well as in maths (when she can write the numbers in order). You can also provide opportunities for your child to:

- draw her own pictures, and/or
- colour pictures within the lines.

The following pages indicate the type of writing and tracing activities your child can practise in Checklist 4.

Writing blends words are an important part of consolidating the process of sounding out words

The child should also be encouraged to sound out blends and write them

Tracing over the focus sentence of the day will assist the child with word identification

Writing her name should be a daily part of the writing activities, and if the child wishes to draw or trace shapes she can continue to do so

Sentence tracing and numbers should be an integral part of the writing activites

I look in any bag.

My book is big.

1 2 3 4 5 6 7 8 9 10

11 12 13 14 15 16 17 18 19 20

Over time it is quite possible for the child to write simple sentences with your assistance

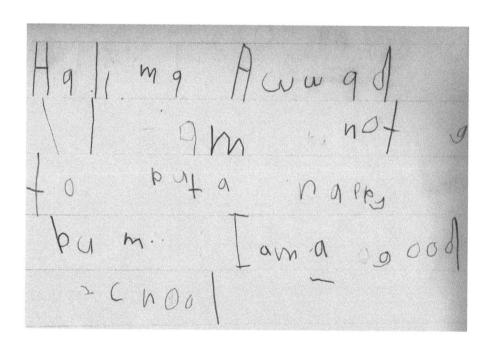

Your child's writing will soon start resembling normal written text

Assist your child to sound out unfamiliar words when writing

In this writing sample the child is experimenting with a texta when writing sentences

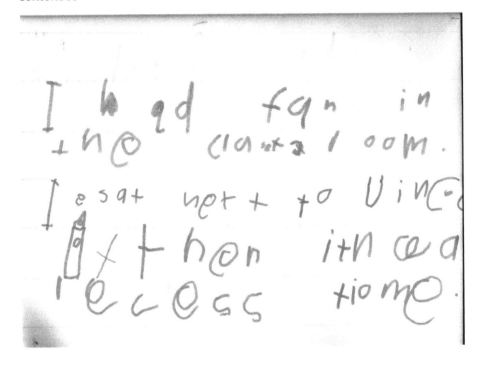

Ruling lines can assist the child organise her work during sentence writing

You may feel that your child is now ready for an A4 exercise book for writing and other activities instead of a large A3 scrap book. If your child has good control of the pencil and the letters produced are legible, now is the time to move on to the traditional exercise book. This will assist the child to make the transition to normal school books, and, over time, she will learn to decrease the size of her writing as she adjusts to the new book size. But if you feel your child's writing is still very large and needs more space, then remain on the A3 scrap book/visual arts diary for as long as needed.

Below are 8 sample copies of how Checklist 4 can be introduced and implemented.

Learning Checklist 4

Day: _Monday_

Date: _19/7_

Write Name	✓
Sentence reading and writing: I have fun on the bike.	✓
Blend focus: an	✓
Raz Kids books/Readers: b	✓
Sight Word focus: I, have, on, the	✓
Writing/tracing (alphabet, numbers, sound out and write blends words, and simple sentences)	

Learning Checklist 4

Day: _Wednesday_

Date: _21/7_

Write Name	✓
Sentence reading and writing: I jump on the trampoline.	✓
Blend focus: en	✓
Raz Kids books/Readers: b	✓
Sight Word focus: jump	✓
Writing/tracing (alphabet, numbers, sound out and write blends words, and simple sentences)	✓

Learning Checklist 4

Day: _Thursday_

Date: _22/7_

Write Name	✓
Sentence reading and writing: I go up and down.	✓
Blend focus: _at_	✓
Raz Kids books/Readers: _b_	✓
Sight Word focus: _go, up, and, down_	✓
Writing/tracing (alphabet, numbers, sound out and write blends words, and simple sentences)	✓

Learning Checklist 4

Day: _Sunday_

Date: _25/7_

Write Name	✓
Sentence reading and writing: I ride on the scooter.	✓
Blend focus: _en_	
Raz Kids books/Readers: _c_	✓
Sight Word focus: revise (I, on, the)	✓
Writing/tracing (alphabet, numbers, sound out and write blends words, and simple sentences)	✓

Learning Checklist 4

Day: _Tuesday_

Date: _27/7_

Write Name	✓
Sentence reading and writing: I play with the ball	✓
Blend focus: ig	✓
Raz Kids books/Readers: c	✓
Sight Word focus: play ,with	✓
Writing/tracing (alphabet, numbers, sound out and write blends words, and simple sentences)	✓

Learning Checklist 4

Day: _Wednesday_

Date: _28/7_

Write Name	✓
Sentence reading and writing: I like to go to the beach.	✓
Blend focus: ot	✓
Raz Kids books/Readers: c	✓
Sight Word focus: like , to	✓
Writing/tracing (alphabet, numbers, sound out and write blends words, and simple sentences)	

Learning Checklist 4

Day: _Friday_

Date: _30/7_

Write Name	✓
Sentence reading and writing: I run on the beach.	✓
Blend focus: in	✓
Raz Kids books/Readers: C	✓
Sight Word focus: revise (I , on, the)	✓
Writing/tracing (alphabet, numbers, sound out and write blends words, and simple sentences)	✓

Learning Checklist 4

Day: _Monday_

Date: _2/8_

Write Name	✓
Sentence reading and writing: We dig with my shovel.	✓
Blend focus: at	✓
Raz Kids books/Readers: C	✓
Sight Word focus: we , my	✓
Writing/tracing (alphabet, numbers, sound out and write blends words, and simple sentences)	✓

Moving on to Kindergarten Workbooks

Now may be the time for you to begin some formal Kindergarten workbook activities with your child. This is a great way for your child to make an easy transition to normal school work. If your child has progressed through the Checklists, she will show you that she is ready for some more challenging work. Notably, it would make sense to start your child on a Kindergarten spelling book, as your child has been practising many spelling skills throughout the Program. Below are some great spelling books that are popular in many schools, and provide many spelling activities to assist your child progress her literacy skills:

- My Spelling Workbook Book A by RIC Publications (AU $9.95) see www.ricgroup.com.au
- New Wave Spelling Book A by RIC Publications (AU $9.95) see www.ricgroup.com.au
- Spelling Rules Book A by Macmillan (AU $13.99) see www.macmillan.com.au

Alternatively, these books can be ordered from your local bookshop, such as Dymocks, or online through a book seller. Due to copyright, it is not possible to show the front cover or inside pages of these books here. However, the website www.ricgroup.com.au has a handy feature which allows you to view all the inside pages of all their books online, before you buy. So check it out if you think your child is ready for formal Kindergarten school work.

Where to Now?

You have put in the time and dedication to teaching your child in the Program. You have sacrificed the time and learned a lot of patience along the way. You have persevered when you thought you couldn't continue any longer. And now your child has progressed to a level you have thought is not possible.

Depending on how long you persevere with the Program, your child will have made considerable progress. She may be:

- Competent in identifying all alphabet sounds, and sounding out simple 3-letter blends, or
- reading and writing basic 3-letters words, or
- well developed in reading and writing, and climbing up the reading levels very fast

You may notice your child will start to observe the world around her in more detail, and attempt to sound and read many words she sees every day. She may notice text around her—at the shops, in the car, on the streets, and will attempt to read the words she sees. This will amaze you.

If you continue with the Program, you will notice that you can start Kindergarten and maybe even Year 1 English, maths and spelling books with your child before her 4th or 5th birthday. It is a real and achievable option.

Whatever your child has achieved so far, you will be faced with an important issue. If your child can identify all alphabet sounds, and can read simple books, or even more challenging ones independently, before she is school age, then you need to think about what this means for your child when she enters school. It may be the case that Kindergarten will be a breeze for her. The fact of the matter is, by the end of Kindergarten, a child should have learned the alphabet sounds, some sight words, and be able to write basic words and sentences. The child should be reading at around level 7, give or take 1. If you have put in the effort during the Program, your child may be well ahead of that reading level when she reaches school age.

You may be faced with the option of skipping your child to Year 1 (which many schools consider after assessing children who are academically bright before they enter school). It's an issue you may have to consider if prompted by the school after assessment of your child.

Or you may have enjoyed the thrills and successes of teaching your child so much that you may be considering another option: to homeschool your child. It's an option that many concerned parents are making for their children, as they recognise that schools can lack in their responsibility to their children, especially academically. You and your child have worked so hard to reach a level where your child can read and write, only for her to enter school and get bored, lose interest, and wait until all of the other children catch up to her, which can take between 1 and 2 wasted years of your child's life. This can be a real issue that parents can face. It is not the intention of this book to recommend homeschooling. However, it is important to investigate the issues you will face after developing your child's academic skills before she enters school.

Chapter 4

Preparing to Implement the Program

You've read all the information about the Program. You are excited and eager to begin, but where do you go from here? Don't get swamped with all the information in all the Checklists and feel that you need to get all the resources for each Checklist ready immediately. It is important to focus on one Checklist at a time.

In order to start the Program, read all the information about Checklist 1 again. Familiarise yourself with what is needed. Photocopy at least 10 copies of Checklist 1 to start off with (from the Index). Or you can first use the Cut-Out copies supplied at the end of the Index. Then gather the required resources, and photocopy what is needed from the Index. Now you are ready to start.

When you feel your child is ready for Checklist 2, read all the information about Checklist 2 again. Have 10 copies ready of Checklist 2, gather the resources, and photocopy what is required from the Index, then begin.

Continue doing this until you reach Checklist 4. Over time you will slowly organise yourself and feel that you are prepared for what is to come.

It is recommended you store all your photocopied Checklists in a plastic sleeve folder or similar file, in order to monitor how many Checklists you have completed and to assist you to decide when it is time to move on to the next Checklist.

All the best with your child's learning!

And remember: the time you invest in your child is what you will get out of her.

Index

This Index has been compiled to help you implement the Program.

In the following pages you will find all the Checklists, proformas of charts and diagrams mentioned in the book.

There are also useful websites that you can refer to for more examples.

In addition, to assist you in starting the Program, 5 Checklists of each type have been included for you to rip out and use straight away.

Below is a summary of what's in each section of the Index.

Summary of Index

ITEM	DESCRIPTION	PAGE NO.
Checklists	These are the 4 Checklists that make up the Program. Use these Checklists to photocopy so you can implement the Program. The size of the Checklists makes it possible for you to photocopy two of the same Checklist and place them side by side. Then you can photocopy two Checklists on one A4 sheet of paper.	189
Rewards Charts	Rewards Charts can be a great way to get your child motivated throughout the Program. Choose the one that you like, photocopy and use, or make up your own using the ones provided as a guide.	193
Correct Formation of Letters	These pages will show you how to correctly write the alphabet so you can assist your child to write them correctly. A general rule is to start from the top down.	195
Pencil Grip	Here you will find an image showing the correct way to hold a pencil. Refer to this page to remind you and your child how to hold the pencil correctly. Pictures of pencil grippers are also provided if you would like to purchase these to assist your child with pencil grip.	196
Sample Tracing Pages	Here you will find samples of pages to photocopy to assist your child with tracing, which will help develop fine motor skills.	198

Sight Word List	There are many Sight Word lists on the internet but the one provided is a simple and basic one to start off with, outlining the most used words in order of difficulty. Use the first words first when choosing sight words to focus on in sentence writing in Checklist 3 and 4.	209
Blends Flashcards	Here you will find the blends words from the Starfall website that your child has been practising from Checklists 2, 3 and 4. You can use these flashcards to revise the blends.	210
Contact Details of Suppliers of Resources	This section will provide you with contact details of suppliers of books and other resources necessary to implement the Program.	217
Websites for Further Resources	Here you will find useful websites you can refer to and print more resources to help you implement the Program.	218
Cut-Out Copies of Checklists	Here you will find 5 copies of each of the Checklists you can cut out and use straight away.	219

CHECKLISTS

<u>Checklist 1 for Alphabet Sounds</u>

Day: _____ Date: _____

Circle letter sounds focused on today

a b c d e f g

h i j k l m n

o p q r s t u

v w x y z

Circle letters child can identify sound off by heart

a b c d e f g

h i j k l m n

o p q r s t u

v w x y z

Learning Checklist 2

Day: _____ Date: _____

Identify Name	
Alphabet Focus: (list letters)	
Blend focus: _____ + Starfall blend activity	
Write blend words: _____ _____ _____ _____	
Raz Kids Online books level:	
Daily Writing/tracing (lines, spirals, shapes, alphabet, numbers, objects)	

Learning Checklist 3

Day: _____ Date: _____

Identify and Trace Name	
Starfall activity blend focus:	
Read and write blend words: _____ _____ _____ _____	
Sentence Reading:	
Raz Kids Online books level: or readers	
Daily Writing/tracing (shapes, objects, letters, numbers, blends words)	

Learning Checklist 4

Day: _____ Date: _____

Write Name	
Sentence reading and writing:	
Blend focus:	
Raz Kids books/Readers:	
Sight Word focus:	
Writing/tracing (alphabet, numbers, sound out and write blends words, and simple sentences)	

REWARDS CHARTS

 REWARDS CHART   Name: _____

Monday				
Tuesday				
Wednesday				
Thursday				
Friday				
Saturday				
Sunday				

Image: digitalart / FreeDigitalPhotos.net

LEARNING CHART

Name: _____

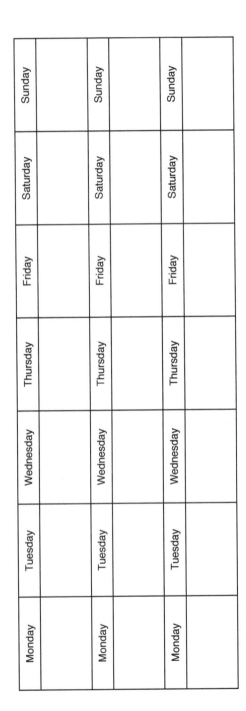

Monday	Tuesday	Wednesday	Thursday	Friday	Saturday	Sunday
Monday	Tuesday	Wednesday	Thursday	Friday	Saturday	Sunday
Monday	Tuesday	Wednesday	Thursday	Friday	Saturday	Sunday

CORRECT LETTER FORMATION

Aa Bb Cc Dd
Ee Ff Gg Hh
Ii Jj Kk Ll
Mm Nn Oo Pp
Qq Rr Ss Tt
Uu Vv Ww Xx
Yy Zz

PENCIL GRIP

PENCIL GRIPPERS

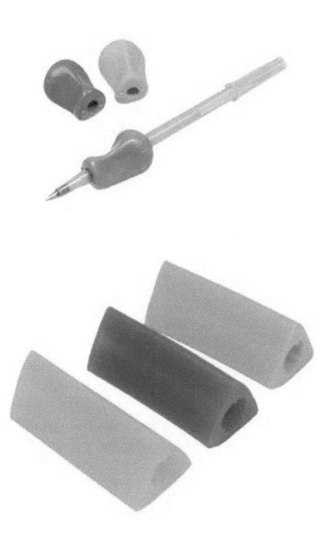

SAMPLE TRACING PAGES

(worksheets copyright of JustMommies.com, reprinted with permission from JustMommies.com)

Trace the rays around the smiling sun and then color the beautiful sun

How many points of sunshine rays can you count?

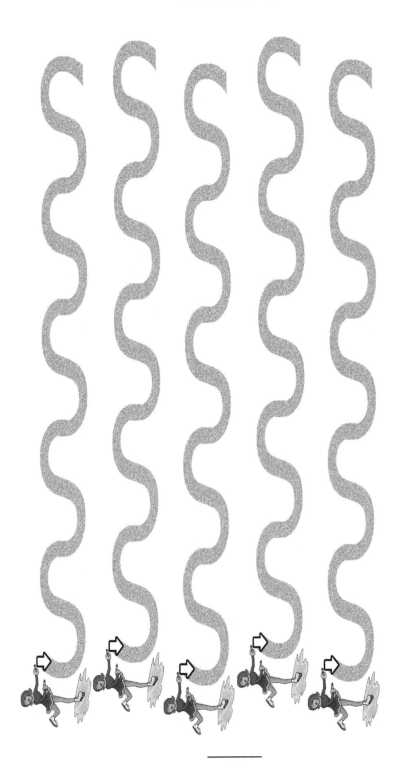

Trace the flower petals and leaves then color the beautiful flower

(worksheets copyright and reprinted with permission from
Printactivities.com)

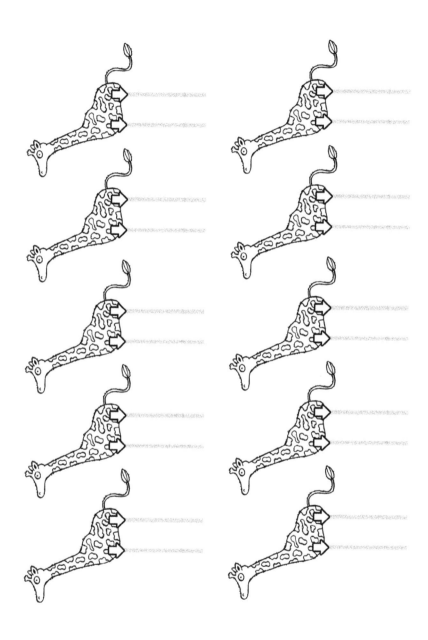

(worksheets copyright of JustMommies.com, reprinted with permission from JustMommies.com)

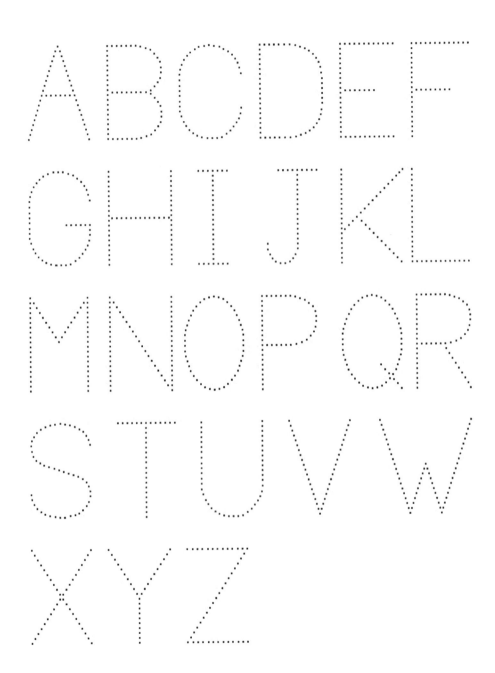

(worksheets copyright and reprinted with permission from Printactivities.com)

(worksheets copyright and reprinted with permission from
Printactivities.com)

Instructions: trace and then copy letters or words

Aa Aa Aa Aa

Aa Aa Aa Aa

Avc otis an apple.

Instructions: trace and then copy letters or words

SIGHT WORD LIST

a	and	away
big	can	come
down	for	go
here	I	in
is	it	jump
like	little	look
make	me	my
not	on	play
run	said	see
the	to	up
we	where	you

BLENDS WORDS FLASH CARDS

cat	fat
rat	hat
bat	mat

mug	bug
rug	hug
pan	ran

fan	can
man	pet
wet	jet

net	men
ten	pen
hen	big

wig	pig
dig	sip
rip	dip

zip	log
dog	fog
frog	hot

pot	cot
dot	lot

CONTACT DETAILS OF SUPPLIERS OF RESOURCES

<u>A3 and A4 Visual Arts Diaries</u>

- Big W, Target, K Mart (in Australia), large reailers, and news-agencies

<u>Sight Words and Alphabet Flash Cards</u>

- Cards sets from the publisher School Zone, which can be found in Big W, Target and online stores

<u>Levelled Readers</u>

- PM+ Readers (mentioned as PM Plus Readers in this book) from Nelson Cengage Learning publishers. To purchase see website http://www.nelsonprimary.com.au/ or to borrow visit your local library and search under the beginning reading section.

<u>My Spelling Workbook Series</u>

- Publisher: RIC Publications (<u>www.ricgroup.com.au</u>)
- Your local educational book supplier may stock the book or order it in for you.
- Other suppliers include Dymocks.

WEBSITES FOR FURTHER RESOURCES

WEBSITES FOR TRACING WORKSHEETS

www.abcteach.com (then click onto PreK/Early Childhood, then Handwriting, then Tracing)

www.kidslearningstation.com (many sections to choose from, but have a close look at Fine Motor link on top of webpage too)

www.kidzone.ws (then click onto Pre-Printing Practice)

www.dltk-teach.com (then click onto Preschool Writing Skills Worksheets)

http://www.shirleys-preschool-activities.com (then click onto Free Printable under Preschool Skills section on the left)

JustMommies.com (Click onto Preschoolers, then Preschooler Education)

www.printactivites.com (then click onto Tracing Worksheets)

www.sparklebox.co.uk/cll/writing/formation/

www.schoolsparks.com/printable-worksheets/category/fine-motor-tracing-lines

www.nationalkindergartenreadiness.com/2011/02/dnealian-alphabet-tracing-worksheets-for-uppercase-letters-a-to-z/

http://ziggityzoom.com/activities.php?c=5 www.kidslearningstation.com

✂
|
|
|

CUT-OUT COPIES OF THE CHECKLISTS

Checklist 1 for Alphabet Sounds

Day: _____ Date: _____

Circle letter sounds focused on today

a b c d e f g

h i j k l m n

o p q r s t u

v w x y z

Circle letters child can identify sound off by heart

a b c d e f g

h i j k l m n

o p q r s t u

v w x y z

Checklist 1 for Alphabet Sounds ✂

Day: _____ Date: _____

Circle letter sounds focused on today

a   b   c   d   e   f   g

h   i   j   k   l   m   n

o   p   q   r   s   t   u

v   w   x   y   z

Circle letters child can identify sound off by heart

a   b   c   d   e   f   g

h   i   j   k   l   m   n

o   p   q   r   s   t   u

v   w   x   y   z

✄ **Checklist 1 for Alphabet Sounds**

Day: _____ Date: _____

Circle letter sounds focused on today

a b c d e f g

h i j k l m n

o p q r s t u

v w x y z

Circle letters child can identify sound off by heart

a b c d e f g

h i j k l m n

o p q r s t u

v w x y z

Checklist 1 for Alphabet Sounds ✂

Day: _____ Date: _____

Circle letter sounds focused on today

a b c d e f g

h i j k l m n

o p q r s t u

v w x y z

Circle letters child can identify sound off by heart

a b c d e f g

h i j k l m n

o p q r s t u

v w x y z

✂ **Checklist 1 for Alphabet Sounds**

Day: _____ Date: _____

Circle letter sounds focused on today

a b c d e f g

h i j k l m n

o p q r s t u

v w x y z

Circle letters child can identify sound off by heart

a b c d e f g

h i j k l m n

o p q r s t u

v w x y z

Learning Checklist 2

Day: _____ Date: _____

Identify Name Alphabet Focus: (list letters)	
Blend focus: _____ + Starfall blend activity	
Write blend words: _____ _____ _____ _____	
Raz Kids Online books level:	
Daily Writing/tracing (lines, spirals, shapes, alphabet, numbers, objects)	

Learning Checklist 2

Day: _____ Date: _____

Identify Name	
Alphabet Focus: (list letters)	
Blend focus: _____ + Starfall blend activity	
Write blend words: _____ _____ _____ _____	
Raz Kids Online books level:	
Daily Writing/tracing (lines, spirals, shapes, alphabet, numbers, objects)	

<u>Learning Checklist 2</u>

✂

Day: _____ Date: _____

Identify Name	
Alphabet Focus: (list letters)	
Blend focus: _____ + Starfall blend activity	
Write blend words: _____ _____ _____ _____	
Raz Kids Online books level:	
Daily Writing/tracing (lines, spirals, shapes, alphabet, numbers, objects)	

<u>Learning Checklist 2</u>

Day: _____ Date: _____

Identify Name	
Alphabet Focus: (list letters)	
Blend focus: _____ + Starfall blend activity	
Write blend words: _____ _____ _____ _____	
Raz Kids Online books level:	
Daily Writing/tracing (lines, spirals, shapes, alphabet, numbers, objects)	

Learning Checklist 2

Day: _____ Date: _____

Identify Name	
Alphabet Focus: (list letters)	
Blend focus: _____ + Starfall blend activity	
Write blend words: _____ _____ _____ _____	
Raz Kids Online books level:	
Daily Writing/tracing (lines, spirals, shapes, alphabet, numbers, objects)	

Learning Checklist 3

Day: _____ Date: _____

Identify and Trace Name	
Starfall activity blend focus:	
Read and write blend words: _____ _____ _____ _____	
Sentence Reading:	
Raz Kids Online books level: or readers	
Daily Writing/tracing (shapes, objects, letters, numbers, blends words)	

Learning Checklist 3

✂

Day: _____ Date: _____

Identify and Trace Name	
Starfall activity blend focus:	
Read and write blend words: _____ _____ _____ _____	
Sentence Reading:	
Raz Kids Online books level: or readers	
Daily Writing/tracing (shapes, objects, letters, numbers, blends words)	

<u>Learning Checklist 3</u>

Day: _____ Date: _____

Identify and Trace Name	
Starfall activity blend focus:	
Read and write blend words: _____ _____ _____ _____	
Sentence Reading: 	
Raz Kids Online books level: or readers	
Daily Writing/tracing (shapes, objects, letters, numbers, blends words)	

<u>Learning Checklist 3</u>

✂

Day: _____ Date: _____

Identify and Trace Name	
Starfall activity blend focus:	
Read and write blend words: _____ _____ _____ _____	
Sentence Reading:	
Raz Kids Online books level: or readers	
Daily Writing/tracing (shapes, objects, letters, numbers, blends words)	

<u>Learning Checklist 3</u>

Day: _____ Date: _____

Identify and Trace Name	
Starfall activity blend focus:	
Read and write blend words: _____ _____ _____ _____	
Sentence Reading:	
Raz Kids Online books level: or readers	
Daily Writing/tracing (shapes, objects, letters, numbers, blends words)	

<u>Learning Checklist 4</u>

Day: _____ Date: _____

Write Name	
Sentence reading and writing:	
Blend focus:	
Raz Kids books/Readers:	
Sight Word focus:	
Writing/tracing (alphabet, numbers, sound out and write blends words, and simple sentences)	

<u>Learning Checklist 4</u>

✂

Day: _____ Date: _____

Write Name	
Sentence reading and writing:	
Blend focus:	
Raz Kids books/Readers:	
Sight Word focus:	
Writing/tracing (alphabet, numbers, sound out and write blends words, and simple sentences)	

<u>Learning Checklist 4</u>

✂

Day: _____ Date: _____

Write Name	
Sentence reading and writing:	
Blend focus:	
Raz Kids books/Readers:	
Sight Word focus:	
Writing/tracing (alphabet, numbers, sound out and write blends words, and simple sentences)	

<u>Learning Checklist 4</u>

Day: _____ Date: _____

Write Name	
Sentence reading and writing:	
Blend focus:	
Raz Kids books/Readers:	
Sight Word focus:	
Writing/tracing (alphabet, numbers, sound out and write blends words, and simple sentences)	

<u>Learning Checklist 4</u>

Day: _____ Date: _____

Write Name	
Sentence reading and writing:	
Blend focus:	
Raz Kids books/Readers:	
Sight Word focus:	
Writing/tracing (alphabet, numbers, sound out and write blends words, and simple sentences)	

Reference List

Anna Gosline. (July 4, 2005). New Scientist Life. In Watching TV harms kids' academic success. Retrieved 4 March, 2011, from *http:// www. newscientist.com/article/dn7626-watching-tv-harms-kids-academic-success.html.*

Fitz Villa Fuerte. (2007). The Importance of Writing Down Your Goals On Paper. In Ready to be Rich. Retrieved February 2, 2011, from *http:// fitzvillafuerte. com/the-importance-of-writing-down-your-goals-on-paper.html.*

Julie Ashton-Townsend. (July 13, 2010). Teaching Phonics - Two Letter Blends. In Ezine Articles. Retrieved June 2, 2011, from *http:// ezinearticles. com/?Teaching-Phonics---Two-Letter-Blends&id=4628021.*

Mary Elizabeth. (June 14, 2011). Sight Words. In Wisegeek. Retrieved July 2, 2011, from *http://www.wisegeek.com/what-are-sight-words.htm.*

Author Biography

Having completed her primary teaching degree, Gheda Ismail embarked on the challenge of establishing her own educational institution, Step Ahead Coaching, in 2004. Now a highly successful tuition centre, Ismail's endeavours have assisted hundreds of primary children achieve their learning goals. After having her first daughter, Halima, in 2007, Ismail wondered how she could go about teaching Halima the fundamentals of literacy at a young age. With no help from any useful books on the market, Ismail decided to create her own Program and trial it out on her daughter, then aged 3. Since then she has not looked back!

Ismail believes that every mother has the potential and capability to implement this proven Program, as long as they have high expectations of their child. And every child can achieve success if they are given the chance!

Lightning Source UK Ltd.
Milton Keynes UK
UKHW010648240519
343267UK00001B/271/P